738.30942

KT-418-992

 **Reading**
BOROUGH COUNCIL

Reading Borough Libraries

Email: info@readinglibraries.org.uk
Website: www.readinglibraries.org.uk

Reading 0118 9015950
Battle 0118 9015100
Caversham 0118 9015103
Palmer Park 0118 9015106
Southcote 0118 9015109
Tilehurst 0118 9015112
Whitley 0118 9015115

REA
RESV 6/06

WITHDRAWN

738.094

0715 367 021 0 166 5C

14 MAY 1975

Pottery in England

Pottery in England
From 3500 BC – AD 1750

K. J. Barton

DAVID & CHARLES
NEWTON ABBOT   LONDON
NORTH POMFRET (VT)   VANCOUVER

0 7153 6702 1

To G. W., J. G. H., G. C. D. — *Satis verborum*

© K. J. Barton 1975

All rights reserved. No part of this publication may be reproduced, stored in a retrieval system, or transmitted, in any form or by any means electronic, mechanical, photocopying, recording or otherwise, without the prior permission of David & Charles (Holdings) Limited

READING PUBLIC LIBRARIES

738.10942

209 Add. 575

Bnd. BARTON

Set in 11 on 13 point Baskerville
and printed in Great Britain
by John Sherratt & Son Limited
for David & Charles (Holdings) Limited
South Devon House Newton Abbot Devon

Published in the United States of America
by David & Charles Inc North Pomfret
Vermont 05053 USA

Published in Canada by
Douglas, David & Charles Limited
3645 McKechnie Drive West Vancouver BC

Contents

List of Illustrations

Plates

In Text

7

Introduction

Pottery is the only man-made material from antiquity that can survive the passage of time unaltered. Fire most clays above 500°C and they will convert to a ceramic that can only be destroyed structurally, by crushing to a powder and dispersing to the winds. Through this special quality ceramic products survive the elements throughout time where all else fails. Each fragment carries its own 'punched card' of information indicating the degree of technical competence used to make it and information on its design and its purpose. Each piece illustrates the domestic, culinary, industrial or religious requirements for which it was especially made. Studied in sequence, they show that man's ability to make pottery has fluctuated through the ages, learning, improving, rejecting or forgetting—never constant, a window on the fickleness of his changing values.

The invention of pottery would seem to be man's first great technical achievement, for it is not a readily achieved thing, like the other primitive crafts that simply adapt natural materials. A considerable degree of technical understanding is required in order to produce a serviceable vessel, and practice is required to control and manipulate the mysteries of what is a complex subject. There have been many periods in man's history when vast areas of the world were without the use of pottery, although it was known elsewhere; at other times, some who did not make pottery used imported wares quite commonly. Potting took a long time to develop, as compared

9

with other crafts, and the reason would seem to be that it took man a long time to realise the possibilities of heat control, which is of the essence in the successful conversion of clay to ceramic: that, and the preparation and quality of the clay to be fired, make pottery. As we know that pottery comes before metal technology, it seems that the techniques of one led naturally to the development of the other.

For well over 5,000 years pottery has been made in England, although it was probably first manufactured in the western hemisphere in Turkey some 4,000 years earlier. Each age, each culture and each cultural sub-division has produced pottery to its own needs, and each has marked its own pottery products with unmistakable characteristics. The growth in the use of pottery has had a very varied pace, and the development of techniques in England has for the most part been slow in comparison with developments on the Continent of Europe. Here the changes have been more abrupt, and sometimes more violent; these have resulted in sharp divisions and, strangely, in better quality. Throughout the periods of potting up to the late eighteenth century AD English products were not only inferior, but appear to have offered nothing to the development of standards, either technically or artistically.

Potting in England began in the Neolithic period, when the settlements of the New Stone Age as it is called were first introduced from the Continent. This occurred about 3,500 BC some 100,000 years after man first came to this land. The first wares were coarse, hand-made and fired in open fires. This method of manufacture persisted for at least 3,000 years, during which time there have been considerable variations in the form, decoration and purpose for which the vessels were made. The first major alteration in technical development occurred about 100 BC with the introduction of the potter's wheel. Although producing mechanically finer vessels, this has had little effect on either the form or the fabric, and—as we see throughout our ceramic history—tradition is hard to break. Even the advent of Rome and its massive technological achievement, so fast and so sudden, made no more impact on the ceramic spectrum, in the short run, than did its road system, its cities or its laws. It was only in the long run, some 500 years after the end of the Roman period, that Roman techniques and some of its pottery forms began to make some impact on the English scene, although when considered as technical products their quality was not to be surpassed until the eighteenth century AD. The strength of the native traditions was persistent and although on occasions modified by outside influences they can be traced back to their Neolithic ancestry; it was only at the end of the Roman occupation that this development was broken. The Saxon settlers, although bearers of a new culture, brought with them a ceramic technique and forms of vessels which were in many respects similar to those commonly made in England 100 years before the Roman invasion. It is with this retrograde step that we take up the threads of development again as if Rome had never been, and the wheel had never been introduced.

The Roman industrial techniques, although abandoned in England, continued and were developed on the Continent, particularly in France and on the Lower Rhine from which source, it is thought, they were reintroduced into East Anglia gradually until by the tenth century AD they were almost as complete there as they had been under the Romans. However, these developments did not become widespread throughout England for another century, but by the thirteenth century, during the period of our first 'industrial revolution', considerable developments took place both in kiln forms and in new ceramic forms. With this development the place of glazed earthenwares became assured and continued until the fifteenth century when a wide variety of changes took place.

The importation of porcelain and the desire to copy it were to the potters as the quest for gold to the alchemist, the effect of this was far-reaching and of great importance to the future of pottery. On top of this there were the importation and subsequent manufacture of tin-glazed earthenwares, commonly called 'delft', during the sixteenth century, and the massive imports of German salt-glazed stonewares, which were also manufactured here from the end of the seventeenth century.

These two activities and the overlying search for porcelain split the earthenware potters into two camps: those who abandoned coarse earthenwares and went to copy the new wares or experimented with finer earthenware, and those who were forced to continue the manufacture of coarse wares in the face of increasing competition. Despite this, the work of the coarse-ware potter managed to continue into the first half of the present century, although thrust deeper and deeper into country places.

The invention of 'creamware' and its subsequent evolution to the ubiquitous 'china' were accomplished on the high crest of the Industrial Revolution, with its chemistry, steam power, factory systems and improved communications. This movement mixed hitherto divided rural and urban communities and threw up new classes whose taste for their recently acquired affluence made demands beyond the capacity of the rural potter. These demands for finer pottery were met with the aid of improved transport, thus sealing the fate of the earthenware potter.

In England throughout historical times up to the advent of Wedgwood potters were treated as vagrants and undesirables, and even the image of Wedgwood has not entirely removed the stigma of oddity attached to what should be considered one of our oldest and most honourable professions.

The developments that are to be discussed here all took place in England proper. What has happened in Scotland, Ireland, Wales and the Western peninsula during many periods was often different, sometimes mirroring England's activities, at other times producing different material, and at others being totally aceramic. In the main, however, ceramic influences have flowed from the south-eastern quarter outwards in slowing ripples, from the Continent to the 'lowland zone' in the southeast and then into the hill country and beyond, so that at some stages the western parts of these islands have been several hundred years behind the latest ceramic stage. For this reason, only the general history of English ceramics can be described, for even this small area is full of complexities, although material relevant to its history from those other areas immediate to England will be included.

Chapter One

The Technical Development

To make a pot you need clay. Having obtained your clay it has to be prepared to a suitable condition to be shaped. Shaped into the required form and dried, it can be 'fired', that is to say, the clay is converted into pottery. These are the four main stages facing the potter of any period.

Clay occurs widely throughout England. It is a by-product of the weathering down of volcanic rocks and in particular the feldspar from these rocks. This breaking down has the ultimate result of removing the alkaline contents of the feldspar, leaving the other main components, silica and aluminas, which with water form pure clay. If this clay when formed is not carried from its source and remains protected it is white, like the deposits in Cornwall and Devon. In such a condition it is known as primary clay. However, such deposits are rare and most clays have been carried by water action, blown by the wind or pushed by ice. These movements add mineral impurities. The commonest impurity in England is iron, which colours the clay in varying shades from cream to the deepest red. Some coal measure clays and others can be stained black with organic inclusions. It is also possible to find clays intermixed with other material such as stones, ranging in size from large boulders down to the finest sand.

If you are to fire your pottery without fully understanding the pyrotechnics, and without the benefit of a controllable kiln chamber, you can fail or have very varied results, for some clays need a higher temperature or a longer firing period than others. In order to control the variations of the clay and the vagaries of the fire, early potters introduced a wide variety of inclusions to the fabric of the vessel as tempering agents. By this means they reduced the amount and thickness of the clay in the body of the vessel, thereby reducing also the time and the temperature needed to convert it to a ceramic. These tempering media were often sand, but flint and stones and any other siliceous or volcanic by-products were used, as was 'grog' (crushed pottery fragments) in some periods. At other times shell, chalk or ground stone were added, and at other times chopped vegetation was used, which burned out in the firing leaving a corky texture to the pot. As stated above, it is of course possible to find deposits of naturally mixed media, such as estuarine clays with a high sand content, or some of the clays into which there has been a washout from limestone, which when fired look as if they have been deliberately tempered although they have not. The materials used in this way often appear to have been selected at random from whatever source might have been available, and often the results of this random selection show in the large and unwieldy pieces of stone added to the vessels. More often, however, the selection appears deliberate even to the extent of crushing or breaking down large items to a uniform and 'selected' size, a feature particularly noticeable in 'flint country' where it would seem that the flints have been roasted and quenched while very hot to produce a fine selection of very small, sharply angled fragments, which are burned through before inclusion in the body of the pot. Recent experiments have shown to some extent that the practice of tempering a pot is unnecessary when firing it in a controllable kiln, but the practice continued in general use up to the fifteenth century and in some instances, such as in North Devon, right up to the nineteenth century.

In the Roman period, and later in the medieval and post-medieval periods when neo-factory systems demanded large quantitites of clay, it was probably dug from pits during the summer and autumn and placed in small heaps where it lay during the winter to be 'frosted' or 'weathered', as it was called by country potters who practised this method of initial preparation during recent historical times. This aided the preparation of the clay by breaking it down and making it more malleable. This natural process was followed by 'puddling' or 'treading' the clay with the feet and it would be at this stage that the tempering agent would be added. This treading was later done using a horse mill, pulling a roller round a trough as in making cider. The clay, thus prepared, would be rolled into large balls and stored in a damp place against use. In the more refined manufactories of the mass-manufacturing periods from the eighteenth century onwards, when relatively high temperatures were used to fire the clay and the ware was un-tempered, further preparation in the form of 'wedging' and 'blunging' were essential. In the first case the prepared clay would be cut up as would a cheese, and one piece would be hurled into the other with some force in order to drive out trapped pockets of air and also to ensure a constant mix to the body. Blunging, derived from the word 'bludgeoning', was simply to take a paddle and beat a lump of clay until the same effect was achieved.

Having prepared the clay in whatevery way is essential to your own requirements you can then make your pot. The ways of making a pot are legion, but there are three principal methods; wholly with the hands (manual); with the hands and some tools (semi-mechanical); and wholly assisted with some rotary actions (mechanical). There are of course a wide variety of variations on all these themes, some of which may be interwoven.

There appear to be two methods of manual manufacture, the 'lump' method and the 'coil' method. In the lump method a vessel is raised using no tools other than a flat surface which has been liberally lubricated with 'slip' (a fine creamy slurry of clay). A ball of prepared clay is pummelled into a cupped shape, placed on to the flat surface and then worked round with the hands, pulling and drawing the upper surfaces, while turning the lump on the wetted surface. This constant rotary action can produce a fine circular vessel. Where this method has been studied the process is seen to be in two stages; the upper portions when completed are allowed to harden to prevent the collapse of the whole vessel, and when this has set the bottom half is finished. This two-part process can cause an imbalance of perfection and the lower portions may never look quite the same as the upper ones, unless the whole vessel is given some surface treatment when it is completely dry. Such imperfections are to be seen on some of the early Saxon coarse wares from both England and north-western Germany.

Coil-building a pot is a method that has been widely, almost universally, used throughout the history of man's work with ceramics. The methods used for this system have been studied all over the world and a wide variety of modifications are known. Some applications are very complex, but the basic method of building a pot is by adding continuous series of layers of clay one on top of the other to produce the desired shape, height, and thickness. To achieve this the prepared clay is pulled from the ball and rolled into long or short lengths, each roll being of the thickness to build the size of vessel required. The rolls are then laid convenient to the place of work, or if the vessel is small and thin in section a roll can be wrapped round the arm to unwind as the pot is raised. The potter works round the vessel which is built up on a flat surface. A disk of clay is laid for the base and the coils are laid and pressed into one another in a circular motion as the pot is built up. As the pot is built the outsides of the coils are dressed and trimmed with the potter's wetted fingers. A skilled coil-builder can achieve a perfectly globular vessel of considerable dimensions, wholly and completely finished without any other mechanical aids. Furthermore, in this method, as the vessel is raised from the base, there is only one operation. Coil-building was used on many of the late Neolithic 'food vessels', beakers, Bronze Age cinerary urns, early Iron Age situlae, Romano-British storage vessels, and other non-standard or large ceramic forms, as also was the case in the Saxo-Norman and medieval periods.

Semi-mechanical methods include using a tool to raise or to

assist in raising a pot. A process which occurs in association with both the lump and coil methods is the use of a batten and can be called the 'hand and batten' method. By this means the vessel is raised by beating the clay from the outside against the clenched fist or the heel of the palm with the aid of bone or a wooden paddle. The lump of clay is fixed to a flat surface so that the potter moves round the vessel beating it into shape, drawing it out as he goes. The batten is, and presumably was, also used sometimes in co-operation with the coil method for finishing and smoothing down the joins.

Another semi-mechanical method is 'slabbing' in which the prepared clay is rolled out on a flat surface and can be treated in exactly the same way as prepared pastry. The sides can be raised to form a dish, or the clay can be cut into wide strips and rolled over a former to make a cylinder, one end of which can be closed with a disk of clay to make a base. Although there are several variables, the flat sheet of clay is not very mobile and this method has limited application. Even though it is one of the simplest to use, its use is apparent in only a few periods, notably in the Roman period and constantly after the Middle Ages, although it might have been used to build the straight-sided, cylindrical-handled beakers of the early Bronze Age.

Semi-mechanical production can also include the finishing of an otherwise manually constructed vessel with the use of a turntable of some undefined type, but one which is not free-wheeling, having to be driven slowly by either the potter or his assistant. There are many examples of vessels which may have been treated in this way, especially during the Middle-Saxon period in East Anglia where the vessels appear to have been rotated, but not quickly enough to make them true. It is also possible to turn a vessel by setting it into a rotatable base such as a large sherd, a round-based stone, a nut husk, or similar object, a practice of many contemporary 'primitive' societies. Perfectly good and well-turned pottery can be produced by this method, with practice and experience. Whether this method was used during the development of English ceramics is not certain, but its possibility should not be ignored.

Mechanical manufacturing methods can be sub-divided into throwing on the wheel, press moulding, spin moulding, and casting. Of these the first to be adopted was throwing on the wheel. By this method the prepared clay is thrown on to a revolving mechanically rotated turntable. The clay is then raised by the hands to form the cylindrical body of the vessel. The methods of spinning the turntable can vary and there is as yet little evidence of how this was done during the early phases of its use. Some medieval illustrations, especially from Western Europe, show potters at a cage of conical shape which was surmounted by the wheelhead and round the base of which was a kicking platform, the whole being suspended on a point at the top of a shaft, set under the wheelhead. It is also probable that some wheels were driven by a counterbalanced fly-wheel of stone or weighted wood which revolved at foot level, driving the shaft set into a pivot in the floor and carrying a wheelhead at its top.

In post-medieval periods we know that one method of propulsion was to have an assistant turn a large fly-wheel, the throwing head being driven at some distance away by a rope-power take-off. In other instances there are indications of the use of water power, in the form of a leet carrying water under the floor of the potter's shed and driving a small water-wheel as a source of power. The mechanical possibilities are as variable as the other facets of this long-practised and infinitely variable trade. Archaeologically, the chances of finding substantial remains of the organic fittings of the potter's shop in England are very remote, although in some of the excavated kiln sites stones with a worn hole in them have been found and called 'pivot stones'.

The introduction of the wheel did not occur until the first century BC and probably arrived either as an influence from Northern France (then Gaul) or directly as a result of the invasions of the Belgic tribes who came from that area. The wheel continued in use throughout the subsequent Roman occupation, after which its use was lost again. It was re-established from the Rhineland to East Anglia at some time in the ninth century, spreading north and west only sporadically and in general having little effect on the whole country until it became generally established by the twelfth century, since which time it has been the universal method of mechanical production.

Press moulding and its associated method, spin moulding, are ways of mass-producing ceramic forms of standard type, such as figurines, ornaments, decorated hollow-ware or the wide variety of odd shapes influenced by metal forms that cannot be thrown. In both instances a mould is made of the required shape, perhaps an open mould, such as a bowl or plate, or a partially closed mould made of interlocking pieces, known as a piece mould. In the case of the open mould this would be spun on the wheelhead and a ball of prepared clay would be thrown into it, pressing into all the convolutions and indentations. The piece mould would be filled manually with pressed clay. The moulds, being made of porous material, take up the water, and the clay matrix as it dries out shrinks, so that when it has dried it can be readily removed. The vessels can then be trimmed up and have other pieces added by adhesion with slip, a process known as 'luting', while still damp enough to work. Such methods as this were commonly used during the Roman period, but after that time not again until the late seventeenth century.

Wet casting is a similar process to piece moulding except that the clay is made into a finely divided creamy slip; this liquid is poured into a piece mould and allowed to stand until much of the water is taken up from sufficient of the slip to totally surround the inside of the mould with a layer of clay. The excess liquid is then poured away, the mould allowed to dry out and the resulting maquette removed. This method was certainly used in the Romano-British potteries for the manufacture of pipeclay figurines and similar small items.

The moulds were made from fired porous clay in the early phases, but the adoption of plaster of paris moulds in the eighteenth century provided a degree of accuracy and mobility that revolutionised pottery production.

Many pottery vessels have handles, spouts, feet, and numerous other fittings. In many cases these fittings are manufactured by hand, and in the case of handles this has been so in all periods, except the Roman and late post-medieval times. Handles are usually pulled, that is, a thick, sausage-shaped piece of clay is pulled downwards and can be given a variety of sectional forms ranging from round to flat. During the Roman period, however, the majority of the handles were rolled out in a double reeded mould, known as a 'dolly box', from which lengths were cut according to requirements. Other fittings were variously made, some of the larger tubular forms being thrown, others formed or pulled by hand, and others press-moulded and then 'sprigged' on the vessel. It is not until the refinements permitted by the use of plaster of paris that the complicated and accurate accessories could be produced.

The development of industrial, agricultural and constructional ceramics cannot be ignored, and it is remarkable that although the end-products of this manufacture are in most ways similar to those of the rest of the ceramic industry, the methods employed were often different. The largest group of forms by far are those produced for constructional purposes and comprise mainly roof furniture, building materials, hearth furniture, floor coverings, and ornamentation. Some pre-Roman building tiles are known from Canterbury, but in the Roman period they occur widely, and again later in ever-growing quantities after the Norman Conquest, although there is some evidence to suggest that a few types were produced during the Saxon period. Whatever the period, the fabric of such material is generally coarser than that used for domestic pottery no matter how coarse (or refined) that may be. The body is heavily tempered with unsorted roughage such as stone, gravel or sand, and the fabric tends to be more roughly prepared than pot body. Fractures show this roughness. Heavy building materials such as bricks, building tiles, flat, hip, gully, or ridge tiles are made in 'formers' such as a bottomless box, as with hand-made bricks today; these were laid on a sand, cloth-covered or plain ceramic bed. In all instances there is one smooth surface where the clay has been wiped off, whereas the side adjacent to the bed is rough. Tiles often bear a mortar key of grooves, made by scoring with the fingers before drying. In the Roman period many tiles and bricks bear the stamp of the Factor. Such items, no matter what the period, are made to a standard. This appears to have been rigidly maintained in the Roman period whereas in the Middle Ages there were deviations which were later controlled by regulations. Where hollow-wares were required these were thrown or coil-built, but even so the fabric remained relatively coarse, as chimney pots, plant pots, bricks and tiles are today.

The use of such materials came into being with the ceramic factories of the legionary potters early in the Roman occupation. The quantity and variety of the production was massive, but this usage died as rapidly as did the rest of the industry with the departure of Roman power and was not reinstated fully and universally until after the Norman Conquest. Roman building materials were also used widely by the Normans, and there is evidence of Saxon floor tiling at York and Winchester, although this was probably made here by continental craftsmen. At Old Sarum the fine cathedral church had ceramic column capitals, and there is sufficient evidence to show a growing specialised trade in this side of the craft in the late Saxon and early Norman periods. The main resurgence came with the industrial turmoil of the thirteenth century, when roof tiles rapidly replaced thatch, stone and slate, even in those areas where the natural product was readily available. By the fourteenth century brick was widely used in the eastern half of England and swept westward to become generally, if not universally, used by the fifteenth century; then in the late seventeenth and eighteenth centuries it became fashionable to have a brick front to one's house, and so the use of brick increased until the impact of newer materials has begun to replace it in the present century.

The use and manufacture of industrial and agricultural ceramics take the same pattern as those of building materials, occurring only during the same periods. The production includes such things as stills (alembics), water pipes, cisterns, urinals, drains, etc, in the Roman period and the Middle Ages, and, from the sixteenth century onwards, growing to a vast and confusing amount of varied equipment by the nineteenth century since which time much has been ousted, first by the production of cheap glass and later by plastics.

Decoration and Glazing

Having prepared the clay and built the pottery object, you can decorate it.

The shape of the vessel and its fittings vary according to the place and period of its manufacture. Curiously, and less logically, so do the decorative motifs which are equally varied through time and space. The varieties and forms of these decorative media are very pertinent to the period and particularity of the vessels produced.

Decorative technique can be divided into six main forms: finger-applied, tool-applied, wheel-turned, applied slips (a very complex series), modelling and glazing.

From the very start of potting in England vessels have been decorated; both finger- and tool-made decoration run side by side from the early Neolithic to the early Bronze Age. The potting decline of the late Bronze Age reduced the decoration to fingerwork, but one notable and short-lived addition in the Hallstatt Iron Age was the use of crushed haematite to give a coloured finish. With the growth of the La Tène Iron Age influence, a high-quality tool-applied decoration became the mode on which was imposed the use of wheel-thrown decoration.

The Roman occupation with its established ceramic history saw the immediate introduction of every form of decoration possible on an earthenware body, with the exception of the use of a blue colour. The whole gamut appears in vast and vulgar form in its early stages, modifying in the middle of the period with the onset of Germano-British slip decoration which provided a series of lively and spirited pots, with the collapse of the industry these were replaced by ceramic forms akin to pre-Roman traditions. These were decorated with a wide form of stampings and other tool-inspired forms, types of decoration which continued right through to the late Saxon period, when finger embellishments return.

The re-introduction of glazing, the wheel and increased production had the effect of stimulating the decoration on vessels which ran riot through the twelfth to fourteenth centuries. After that came a phase of modest decoration which comprises some slipwares and a little glazing, or one or two highly specialised forms of regional decoration, and so on up to the end of the sixteenth century when once again slip decoration became fashionable and in many areas ran riot right up to the middle of the eighteenth century. At the end of the sixteenth century the introduction of delft (tin-glazed earthenware) added to the decorative scene a form that was of importance throughout the seventeenth and early eighteenth centuries. To some extent salt-glazed stoneware had a part in the use of new decorative media after the end of the seventeenth century. Its association with the 'fine earthenware' developers led to the development of finer decorative techniques, such as sprigging, printing and transfer work that were commonplace through the two ensuing centuries. These late developments continued in use until the Anglo-Nipponese school of potters of the present century liberated thought on the subject, and new forms of decoration are now commonly seen not only on 'art' pottery but on commonly used products.

Glazing should be considered as a form of decoration, for on most earthenwares, and particularly on those of early periods, it remains porous no matter whether the vessel is glazed inside or outside or on both sides together. Although the glaze may act as a temporary seal, water will percolate through even the finest and most recent of relatively hard-fired examples.

Three types of glazing occur: lead-glazing, tin-glazing and salt-glazing. Tin-glazing is a by-product of lead-glazing, but salt-glazing is a separate method. Both tin-glazing and salt-glazing are of post-medieval date as far as production in England is concerned.

Lead-glazing is undertaken by preparing a litharge of galena (lead ore) by grinding. There is some evidence to show that, at least in the Middle Ages, the ore was roasted, which fractured the ore and eased the grinding process. The ore was ground or milled into a fine powder and was applied to the vessel in various ways. It was either dry-dusted through a bag on to the wet surface of a newly made pot, or mixed with a slip into which the pot was dipped, or applied with a brush as a slurry of lead and clay. Whatever the method used, and all appear to have been used throughout the period of lead-glazing, the object was to get the lead to stick to the pot before and during the drying-out period and during the firing before it fluxed. At a given temperature, dependent on the quality of the lead, the type of clay, the tempering from which the pot was made and the temperature of the fire, the lead melts and will flux with the silicas on the outside of the body of the vessel, producing a glaze, which gives a cover of a lead/silica glass.

The colour of a lead glaze can be influenced by its purity. Refined lead without impurities can and does produce utterly clear glazes, and these are seen in antiquity, but mostly on imported material before the post-medieval period. The glaze can also be coloured by mineral additives. However, the use of untreated glaze can provide a wide spectrum of colours on its own account. The colour of an unpurified lead glaze is predominantly yellow; if the glaze is fired in an oxidising atmosphere on a body that contains no iron whatsoever, such as a white fabric, the glaze colour will be yellow. If the body is rich in iron (which is the commonest type) and is fired in an oxidising atmosphere, the resultant body colour will be in shades of red, depending on the amount of iron present, and these shades will be reflected in the glaze colour which will range from orange to brown accordingly. The effects of reduction in a kiln produce a wider variety but only on iron-rich fabrics, for if an iron-free body with a lead glaze is fired in a reducing atmosphere this will result in a dirty grey colour to the glaze. For this reason iron-free clays are almost always fired oxidised or have their firing terminated with oxidisation. Should an iron-rich body be fired with a lead glaze in a reducing atmosphere, the fabric of the body will be grey and the glaze green, what is known as 'reduced iron green'. Examined against a true green, say a copper green, it is seen to be near shades of brown, but the general effect is of a green finish.

Glazing was used during the Romano-British period. Fine lead-glazed pots were imported; the home product was perhaps less than 1 per cent of the whole and was not of very good quality. Glazing, like much else, was re-introduced during the tenth century. It is not known whether this was an English or French re-discovery, as the initial glazing of pottery vessel occurs in these countries consecutively, although it was probably a continental innovation as the standard forms and the general technology of that region were generally in advance of our own. Lead-glazing became generally widespread after the end of the twelfth century and continued unabated and generalised through history to the present day, when its use has been greatly restricted by health regulations. On this sad note ends the history of what has undoubtedly been the most versatile of ceramic finishing media and one that gave the most satisfying of all results when properly applied.

A technical weakness of lead-glazing that was not appreciated for some 400 years after its re-introduction is that when glaze fluxes it runs, and if there is an excess, as there frequently was, the run glaze will stick to whatever the pot is stood upon. This sticking can lead to a great loss of pots, but it can be prevented by the use of kiln furniture, such as sand, kiln props or saggers. Kiln props are pieces of clay often of conical shape on which the pot can be stood away from its neighbour. Since the introduction of casting techniques the variety of these props has increased tremendously but the basic principle of raising the vessel on a sharp point remains the same; the use of these can be detected on some examples of modern earthenware. Vessels can be stood on sand as a separator, but only if the vessel has something wide or dish-shaped to stand in. The method eventually achieved as being the best for the separation of vessels is the 'sagger'. These are large, cylindrical vessels, with or without holes in the side, in which an individual pot can be stood on props or in sand. The saggers are then stacked up in the kiln, separating pot from pot and guaranteeing less wastage.

It really is quite remarkable that such separating techniques were not used until an advanced stage in the history of English potting. There is no evidence of the use of saggers before the sixteenth century, although there are a few indications of kiln props before that time. As a result thousands of glazed pots were 'wasted' through sticking together, and the commonest find on any medieval or early post-medieval kiln site are the stuck tops and bottoms of jugs. The introduction of saggers took as long to spread as did other ideas, and in some more remote places the old-fashioned method persisted until the nineteenth century. This aspect of potter economy, the inability to understand the problems of what should have been a major feature in the production of wares, is puzzling considering the stereotyped view of the peasant as shrewd and niggardly.

Kilns

Having prepared your clay, made your pot, added the fittings and decorated it, you must now convert it by heat from clay to ceramics.

First of all the vessel must be thoroughly dry, as dry as is possible, and the drying process must be carefully undertaken; if it is carelessly done, the vessel will crack and break up before it can be fired, or will break up in the kiln. The principal reason for this careful drying is to remove any trapped moisture which would convert into steam in the kiln, blowing the pot asunder.

Pots can be fired in structural (contructed) kilns or in non-structural kilns, and these two methods have sub-divisions. The non-structural variety are known as 'clamp' or 'clump' kilns, which are either oxidising or reducing kilns, the results achieved requiring different techniques. The structural types are classified as single-flue updraught, double-flue updraught, parallel flue, multi-flue updraught and down-draught.

In all kilns one of two forms of finish is always aimed for (though not always achieved). These are an oxidised finish or a reduced finish. Oxidisation is achieved by allowing a free passage of air round the vessel while it is being fired. This air burns away all the carbons, and when controlled will produce a bright red colour all through an iron-rich fabric, while an iron-free fabric will be white all through. In reduction the passage of air is restricted and so the flammable materials are starved of oxygen and remain as carbon. Carbon from the firing process can also be absorbed by the fabric. This will produce a grey or totally black fabric if iron is present, while if no iron is present the colour will range from off-white to grey. The reduction of wares was common to many periods.

The failure to find structural kilns of pre-Roman times (although one has been tentatively identified for the neolithic period in Scotland) indicates that pottery was fired in clamps. The clamp was probably, in its early stages at least, a small open fire of wood, peat or other combustible material sufficient to fire a single pot or a small group of wares. These fires of mixed fuel would burn rapidly and give a lot of free oxygen, and when firing was completed the vessels were probably covered with the embers to cool; these embers, having free air round them, would burn to a white ash, as does any free bonfire, leaving the vessels with a dull buff to red finish of the type that we see in the earliest vessels of our history. This finish is common to both early and secondary Neolithic vessels, where there is some evidence of irregularity of fire control as the finish on many vessels is dull, and in the secondary Neolithic is often nearly reduced. In the Beaker period which followed, the quality is far superior. Although the firing was carried out in a relatively uncontrolled fire, there is sufficient evidence in the quality of the finish to suggest some special measure of control in the form of a purpose-built clamp. This ability to control the fire became widespread throughout England and Ireland and persisted into the middle Bronze Age. There followed a long period of decline through the rest of the Bronze Age and up to the second phase of the Iron Age. During this decline pots were fired in oxidising clamps that produced a low temperature. The vessels can range in colour from dull grey to a chestnut brown. Their fabric is poor and often very soft. Buried under permanently damp conditions, the pottery when found is seen to have disintegrated. Here is a combination of bad construction and poor firing, a decline further illustrated by the poor design of the period.

The La Tène Iron Age, famous in other fields for its advances in both art forms and military defensive systems, seems also to have been responsible for the introduction or the development of the reducing clamp kiln. In this period we have the totally reduced pot which is black all through, a form of pot colouring that was to remain throughout the ensuing 250 years of the Iron Age, the 400 years of the Roman occupation, for 200 years of the Saxon period and sporadically onwards through to the sixteenth century in one form or another. It must be assumed that to achieve a vessel that is black not only on its surfaces but right through, the fabric requires a clamp kiln of special construction. I suggest that the nearest parallel to such a kiln would be the autumn bonfire of the kind that fills the October nights with white and acrid smoke. These burn very slowly, although the heat produced is the same or has the same firing ability as the open clamp. The achievement of an all-black pot by this method can be readily proved simply by placing a plant-pot (ceramic) inside a bonfire, ensuring that it will not be exposed when the fire burns down; it will come out black all through.

The archaeologist has searched in vain for such kilns and so far no site that could be proved as a 'clamp' of prehistoric date has been published. This is understandable in as much as the fabrics fired by these methods were soft and would probably not warp or overfire to a very hard state as occurs in structural kilns. It is also possible that there were no major centres of production where wasters could be found in abundance, although it has recently been suggested that there was some form of manufactory in commercial production in the Malvern Hills during the Hallstatt Iron Age.

The structural kiln was imported as a part of the Roman industrial traditions. The Romans brought two forms of kiln with them, the single-flue updraught and the parallel-flue. Both forms are well-developed structures of considerable antiquity, for they were in use by the Greeks at least as early as the fifth century BC, and as they were developed then it can be assumed that they go farther back in time than that. Their ability as competent technical structures is acclaimed by the fact that the single-flue updraught kiln continued in use until the eighteenth century, while the parallel-flue kiln remains in use unchanged in the brickfields of twentieth century England.

The single-flue updraught kiln was constructed by excavating a circular expansion chamber with a square-sectioned flue trench to one side terminating at a wide and shallow stoke-hole. Within the expansion chamber was a column made of clay tiles or of stone carried up to ground level where was set a radial of fired clay bars upon which the vessels were stood. The kiln was covered with a clay dome, which could be coil-built or raised on a wicker framework. In the centre of this dome was the vent-hole; the flue was also covered in with a clay roof. When the kiln was stacked, fire was made in the stoke-hole and the heat was carried through the flue into the expansion chamber, rising through the vessels and escaping through the vent.

This simple description is not enough to give full details of the variations of Roman kiln types so far discovered, for, as in other periods, they are as diverse as the number of kilns known. One has only to consider the varieties of Roman kilns found at Colchester to see this, and although there are one or two double-flue updraught kilns published as Roman, the principal form of construction remains the same, an updraught kiln, with one stoke-hole and flue, an expansion chamber, some varied form of support for the floor of the kiln, and a fixed or temporary dome. Such a definition would apply equally to the large kilns of the legionary factories or some remote kiln on the Somerset levels or the Derbyshire Peak.

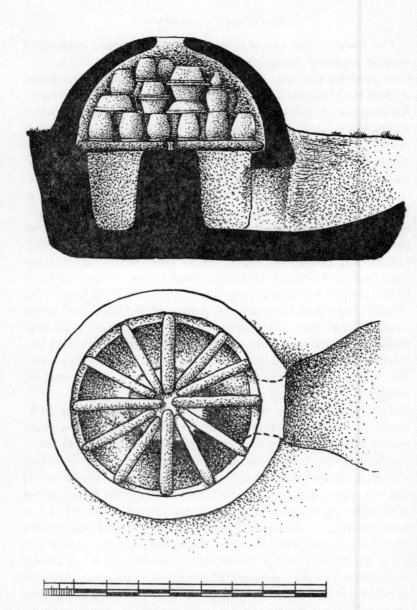

Single flue updraught kiln. Romano-British example.

The parallel-flue kiln was designed to fire heavy ceramics, such as building materials (although at various times it has been used for pottery, and building materials have been fired in updraught kilns). This type of kiln is built upon the surface. Rectangular in form, it consists of a series of single or double arches built side by side in a series to form a single or double tunnel. These arches, constructed in brick or tile, are spaced about 15 cm apart and are surrounded on three sides with walls; the two side walls are raised to a barrel vault and the rear wall seals the end. The front is left open until the kiln is loaded, when a wall is built up using fireclay as a mortar. The top of the vault is vented. The kilns are stacked to allow a free passage of heat, the fire being generated directly in the tunnel underneath the slatted floor. Such kilns would demand a considerable amount of fuel and would therefore be devoted to the mass firing of heavy ceramics.

Such kilns, lost after the departure of the Romans, were reintroduced into England from the Continent probably during the thirteenth century, when they were mainly used for the production of tiles, bricks, flooring materials etc; they were also to influence the type of pottery kiln in at least one part of England.

The reintroduction of the single-flue updraught kiln took place at some time during the seventh century, and was mostly an East Anglian feature. These reintroduced types were less sophisticated than the Roman forms, some merely being scrapes in the ground. Others were dug out of banks and covered over in parts leaving a top vent and a bottom flue giving on to a chamber in which the pottery lay unsupported. Refinements were developed, however, and by the tenth century, at the great potting centre of Thetford, there was a marked constructional form, with complex kiln bars in which pottery of a very high standard was produced. The truth is that our knowledge of the early development of kilns is slight, but growing. One problem is that the kilns of this period so far discovered are mainly situated in East Anglia and, although there is by now evidence of good-quality potting requiring kilns at other places,

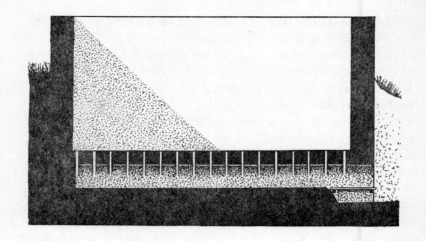

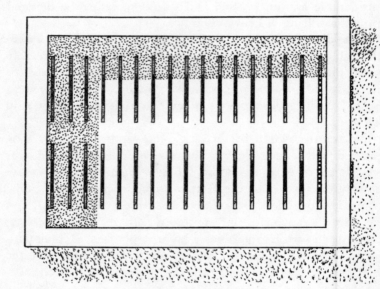

Parallel flue updraught kiln.

Page 33 Neolithic Windmill Hill types: (*above*) from a 'causewayed camp' at Staines, Middlesex. (*below*) from Hesterton, Yorkshire; (*centre*) two spoons from Hassocks, Sussex; (*below right*) from North Bavant, Wiltshire.

Page 34 (above) Neolithic Peterborough ware. A group of various vessels showing the principal form of bowl decoration and two variations.
(upper left) From Hedson; *(right)* from Mortlake; *(lower left)* from Wallingford; *(centre)* from Ebbsfleet. *(left)* Late Neolithic/Early Bronze Age beaker. Decorated entirely with impressed cord. Norham Castle, Northumberland

the kilns are yet to be found. The life of single-flue kilns is very long. They have recently been found in association with other forms of medieval kilns in the Midlands. In the same area one large and one small example were found in association that produced fine wares of early eighteenth century date, and there is a record of a similar type being used in Wiltshire up to the early part of the twentieth century.

In the thirteenth century three types of kiln were in common use throughout England. The spread of the use of pottery kilns appears to have been very rapid in this period and co-relates to the minor 'industrial revolution' that brought in the post-mill and tilt hammer. The three forms comprise the double-flue updraught kiln, the multi-flue kiln and the parallel-flue kiln which has already been described.

The double-flue updraught kiln is merely an enlargement of the single-flue type. It is usually an oval trench 12–15 ft long with a rectangular flue trench at each end, the flues terminating in shallow stoke-holes. The internal fittings vary considerably from region to region and from period to period. In Cheshire there are no central fittings, in Somerset a single baffle wall, in Wiltshire a raised platform, and so on, so that the same can be said of medieval kilns as was said of Roman kilns, that there are as many variations as there are kilns known. However, the difference between the Roman and the medieval types is significant, for in the latter there is in general no combustion chamber—although even these are known in at least two places. The lack of combustion chamber means that the wares were fired in direct contact with the fire and without the benefit of completely controlled heat. Support for the vessels was apparently negligible; in one or two instances kiln bars were used, or the vessels were laid in pottery cradles, but in most they were stacked on the floor or supported slightly off it on stones. Whatever the methods used in this period, the outcome is remarkably similar, no matter how sophisticated or otherwise the kiln may be.

The double-flue updraught kiln lived on, as far as we know, well into the seventeenth century, and like its forebear the single-flue kiln appears to have been surplanted by the multi-flue kiln only in the closing years of the seventeenth century. Its use as a temporary structure did apparently continue, however, as a potter working at Clevedon, Somerset, at the turn of the twentieth century was taught as an apprentice to construct such kilns for the firing of special 'biscuit' pieces; the 'glost' firing was done in an updraught kiln.

Such double-flue updraught kilns occur mainly south of the Trent. Above this line the distribution is less obvious, and in Sussex, excluding Chichester, and perhaps in Kent also, there is another variety. The source for double-flue kilns has recently been sought in the area of south-western France known as the Saintonge which was rich in material exported to Britain in the Middle Ages, but the kilns here were found to be of the parallel-flue type. However, the kilns at Andenne in Belgium are of double-flued form.

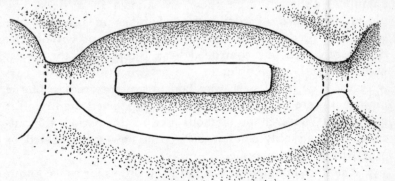

Double flue updraught kiln. Medieval type.

One of the most important, if not the most important, factor in the history of Western European ceramics was the creation of the multi-flue up-draught kiln. These kilns occur as early as the thirteenth century, mostly in the area defined by the counties of South Yorkshire, Nottinghamshire, Derbyshire, Staffordshire, South Lancashire and Lincolnshire. By this period such kilns were already abundant round the old and new settlements of this growing area, and recent work has shown that they were distributed at a distance of about ten miles from one another. The kilns are circular in structure, some 10–15 ft across, built on or slightly below the ground and having a thick clay floor. At five or more points there are entries to this floor, in the form of rectangular flues extending radially outwards from the edge of the floor to well-defined stoke-holes. One of the entries is usually without a flue and is often just a hollow way, the kiln floor showing the dirt of trampling, and this must have been the walk-in used for stacking the kilns. Such walk-ins suggest that the earliest of these kilns was equipped with some permanent or semi-permanent structure. This type of kiln has very little in the way of major variations, although of course some have been noted. In many cases the kilns persisted on the same site for many centuries; examples have been found that have been destroyed and rebuilt as much as fifteen times, and during use some minor modifications have also taken place. The basic design remains constant, however, in that these kilns, being circular in shape and of reasonably large dimensions, must have had a large dome raised over them of sufficient size for a man to enter either walking or crawling. The pottery fired in these kilns was in the earliest period unprotected and placed directly on the floor of the kiln without supports. The whole was fired through the radial flues at one time, and the heat was directed through a vent or possibly through some form of stack pipe.

The covering of kilns will be discussed below, but in this instance the situation is of special importance, for the history of this type of kiln is long and in its later stages, at least by the seventeenth century, kilns of this type are known to have had

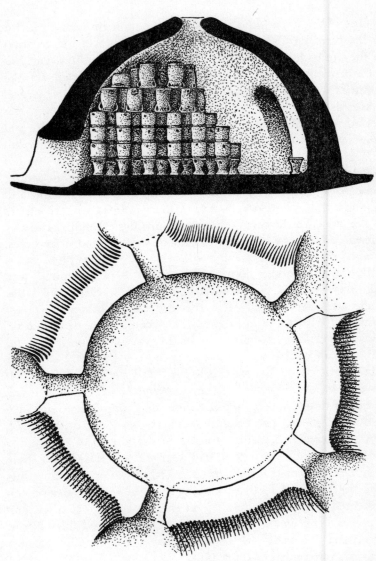

Multiflue updraught kiln. Early post-medieval.

a permanent structure of stone or brick. These structures, probably relatively low in height, have by this time reached the 'bottle' shape, so commonly seen on illustrations of kilns in the eighteenth century, and by this time they were universal throughout England and areas beyond. By the nineteenth century they had become massive in size. Up to 80 ft in height, built of red brick and bound with great hoops of iron, they came to dominate the five towns that make up Stoke-on-Trent, filling it with the black monuments of the Industrial Revolution. This kiln form was adopted by glass-makers, maltsters, hop-roasters, and iron-masters, and so some are still used to this day—but no longer by the potter who has replaced them with gas and electricity, while government has damned them with Clean Air Acts.

The medieval kilns of Sussex (excepting one at Chichester) are the odd men out in this story, for they are a separate form constructed on the lines of the parallel-flue kiln. Such kilns occur at Binstead, Rye, Hastings and Ringmer, a range that may well extend into West Kent. These kilns are about 8ft long by 4ft wide, rectangular in shape, and may have a squared or rounded back. There is a central spine wall dividing the rectangle and creating two flues from which spring a series of arches carrying a slatted floor on which the pots were stood, giving an expansion chamber underneath. At Rye there appear to have been secondary chambers to this structure, probably used as drying ovens. Rye, however, is exceptional for the quality and variety of its pots, and we may well see here another example of many variables that are related to the skill and personality of the potter rather than an indication of kiln development *per se*. Such kilns as the Sussex type are of interest as they are certainly a direct descendant of the parallel-flue kiln, and indeed the Binstead example was working adjacent to such a kiln. If we assume the parallel-flue kiln to be a thirteenth century innovation, the Sussex examples can be no earlier, and indeed should be of later date.

So far no mention has been made of the methods used in the covering of medieval kilns. We know that most Romano-

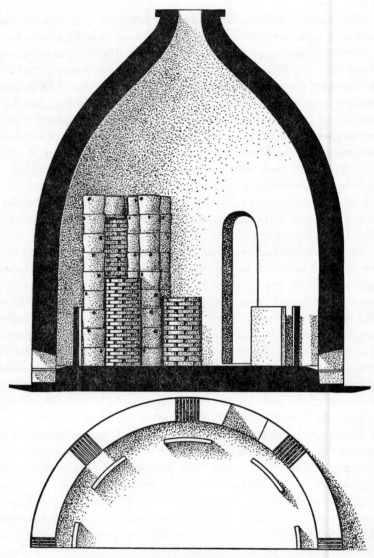

Multiflue updraught (Bottle kiln), 18th/19th century.

British kilns were covered with a clay dome, and that by the sixteenth century multi-flue updraught kilns had perman ent coverings, but as yet there is no corpus of reliable evidenc e to show that medieval kilns were covered, which they mus t of course have been. If a kiln is covered with a clay dome, of no matter what thickness, some if not all of that dome woul d be converted to cera:nics by the same heat that converted the pottery below it. Should this be the case, remains of part o f the baked cover would be found, as is often the case with Rom ano-British kilns—but there is little record of such cove ring material found on medieval kiln sites. Two such kilns rece ntly excavated, one at Knighton on the Isle of Wight and the ot h er at Chichester, were carefully examined with this problem in mind. No baked cover was found, but in each kiln there were examples of 'cob', a mixture of chalk and clay commonly u sed for wall building in the south-west of England. To burn such a mixture would convert the chalk into quicklime, which would in turn slake when wetted under buried conditions, thus destroy ing the structure. However, such a material would be admira ble for building a coil dome which would break down easily after the firing. This is one possible explanation. In other areas the expedient of building the pots into a pattern suitable to allow a passage of heat on the inside, then covering the structure with turves or soil or other similar material would suffice. Such a method is used in Chateauroux, in France, to this day, where fine, large, fully oxydised pottery is produced. The truth must be that potters in different areas used a wide variety of coverings, and that none that we know of were permanent, at least during the early part of the Middle Ages.

At some time, as yet undetermined, during the eighteenth century the down-draught kiln was either developed or intro-duced from some outside source. Such kilns are similar in shape to bottle kilns without the chimney on top. The dome shape has a large, round vent-hole in the top; in the centre of the floor directly under this vent is another vent of equal size which gives into a tunnel. This tunnel passes underneath the floor and beyond the area of the kiln for some distance, when it

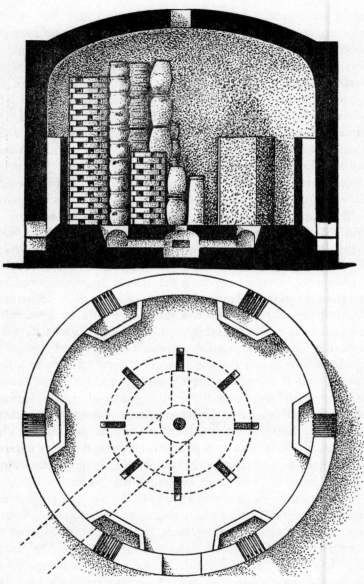

Down draught kiln (18th/19th century). Tunnel shown by dotted lines.

rises to the base of a tall chimney. These chimneys, being between 8oft and 1ooft in height, create a natural updraught which draws air down through the vent in the kiln dome. The flues are placed radially as in the multi-flue kiln, with, of course, a walk-in for stacking purposes. Within the curved walls of the kiln is another similar wall creating a double skin, known as a baffle wall. Its purpose is to ensure that the heat from the fires is drawn upwards towards the vent-hole, from which position it is drawn down through the wares stacked across the floor, eventually through the flue vent and up the chimney. By this means two advantages are achieved: direct loss of heat going straight up the chimney is avoided, and a regular and better controlled draught is ensured. Such kilns had an appeal in potteries where high temperatures were desired, and they were used extensively in the production of stonewares and heavy industrial and domestic ceramics. They are still used for brick and tile making and for the salt-glazed pipe trade.

The fuel required for making pottery depends upon the number of pots, their size and the method used for firing. Almost anything combustible, if there is enough of it, will raise the temperature to a sufficiency if correctly used. We assume that in prehistoric times wood was the principal fuel, although there is ample evidence to show that peat was used as well.

In structural kilns wood is the commonest form of fuel, although in Roman times coal is known to have been used, though not to the same extent. The medieval potter used whatever material was to hand, and all manner of kilns were fired with wood, coal and peat and sometimes some of each. It was not until the end of the seventeenth century that cheap and readily available coal was used for general firing. Many of the later kiln sites are set on coalfields, such as Buckley, North Wales; Sunderland. South Yorks–Nottingham, Ewenny, Swansea and Bristol; or near to ports where coal was readily shipped, such as London (south bank), Liverpool (Herculanium, a coaling dock), Lowestoft, Glasgow, Dublin and Belfast; or again in deep forest removed from populations but not from the essential fuels, such as Boresford (Herefordshire), Potters-bury (Northants), and Harlow (Essex). The demands of rising populations, changing tastes and foreign competition meant big business for the potter, who in his turn made considerable demands on fuel.

When all is done and the pot is fired, a period of cooling takes place and then the moment of truth is realised when the kiln is finally opened, for the vagaries of potting are exemplified in the ultimate outcome of the finished product. The chances of failure are many—wet ware; badly prepared body; the use of a slip or glaze that will not marry with the pot; badly set fittings; the wrong slip for luting; bad stacking or no allowance for natural movement, causing a crash; and, worst of all, bad kiln control causing excessive or insufficient heat; and at least a dozen other disasters that can occur in the confines of a white-hot chamber where nothing can be done about it.

The Economy of Potting

No matter what process of pottery manufacture is used, if it is practised often enough a speed and skill will be acquired that can produce a quality of perfection unequalled by those whose practice is casual. A good quality of pottery production should therefore be indicative of a general state of high technical ability. However, throughout the history of English potting the quality has varied tremendously from period to period. Arbitrary time boundaries suggest that competent potting was practised in the following periods: early Neolithic, some late Neolithic, Beaker, early Bronze Age, Hallstatt Iron Age, La Tène Iron Age, Belgic Iron Age, Romano–British, early Pagan Saxon (funerary urns), Saxo–Norman in East Anglia, the Middle Ages and onwards. The pottery of other periods is indifferent, as in the secondary Neolithic, mid to late Bronze Age, most Saxon, immediate post-Norman to medieval, and earthenwares after AD 1800. It could be argued that these boundaries are too arbitrary, but they are a general guide to the principal argument.

The existence of these two groups of periods must be significant, and there is in them a suggestion that there may be trader potter and casual potter economies at work.

Three kinds of situation can occur, some of them within one period of our time scale: an aceramic economy, a casual potter economy, and a trader potter economy. As an example of the first, we know of large areas of this country where pottery was not used while it was being used elsewhere—for instance in the Neolithic when the tradition was spreading, the Welsh hill forts in the Iron Age, the Celtic West from the seventh to the tenth centuries, the Welsh marches in the early Middle Ages, etc.

Casual potters are only slightly removed from this sphere, making pottery for occasional use such as storage jars or funerary vessels, as in the middle Bronze Age or the Hallstatt Iron Age. The last examples are those wares made in the eighteenth century in Ireland and Scotland of incredible crudity equal only to poor-quality Bronze Age pottery, found in association with fine-quality salt-glaze wares. These potters made wares for immediate and personal use. They were not affected by the need to trade, the need to make a living from their product, or therefore to care about quality, quantity production, or, above all, competition. Even in those periods where trader potters existed, there still remained the individual local potter serving a limited community whose product was individual—often poor—and very limited in range.

A trader potter economy is related to a constant skill acquired through practice and in the face of demand and competition. This should and often does lead to improved technical competence (but not always to understanding). If this is the case, then all those periods in which good-quality pottery was produced (in relation to the standards of development at the time) must have had trader potter economies, and other periods casual potter economies.

The work of an individual or group of individuals can be recognised, and the distribution of the products studied. To this end the regional variations of the secondary Neolithic,

Beaker and Bronze Age, Hallstatt and La Tène Iron Age, some kiln products of the Roman period, the work of a maker of Saxon funerary vessels, the products of the late Saxon potting centres in East Anglia, and the distribution of wares from specific medieval kilns have been studied.

The distribution of the products of a potter seems to fall into two types, strictly local or over a very wide area. Under Roman military rule chance distribution was less, as there is evidence of orders for pots to be made for quartermasters and pottery has been found on the Wall which originated in Derbyshire and Lincolnshire. A similar situation probably occurred in the Middle Ages, where the Ham Green (Bristol) products turn up in castles and religious houses throughout South Wales, and in Dublin, one-time colonial outpost of the city of Bristol. In the seventeenth century, by virtue of the old colonial practice of restricting manufacture, pottery was shipped from the whole extent of the West Country to the colonies or to anyone else who would care to buy it. These major distributions, though common enough, did not supply the bread and butter business of the potter, the bulk of whose product went to the weekly market, the monthly fair or its equivalent, a distribution of about twenty miles. Special orders would be made to be carried any distance. The bulk distribution would also be further spread by middlemen, hawkers and the like, of any period. Pots can also travel far if used as containers for something else. An instance of basically local distribution is that of the Binstead, Sussex, potters whose wares can be found over an area fifty miles long by thirty miles wide; on the periphery of this arc, examples are few indeed, and the bulk of the wares is to be found within ten miles of the kiln site. In the Iron Age pottery was made on the Malvern Hills in Worcestershire and traded over a wide area of the West Midlands, but again the bulk is found nearest to the source. The same rules surely apply to the majority of trader potter goods, as there appears throughout England during any of these periods a similar distribution of types.

One further aspect to be considered is the regional variations

46

of pottery design. The density of these variations is related, of course, to the settlement of the populations, but in any culture pottery forms, fittings and decorations are likely to show local-ised forms. Examples of, say, the Bronze Age overhanging rimmed urn may be found widely in the British Isles, and their form will be the same in whatever locality. However, the size and the decoration of those from different areas will not be the same, and in many cases will differ considerably. In all of the more localised—say, the more primitive—cultures this could perhaps be expected, but even in the case of Roman pottery where at first sight the wares to be seen in all England and Gaul together appear similar, closer examination will show that each individual local potter treated his wares somewhat differently. In this period and in the Saxon and medieval periods such close contacts with Western Europe were main-tained, and still the variations appear and are self-evident. The post-medieval period saw the breakdown of this link of styles, which was not resumed until the arrival of the ubiqui-tous cup and saucer, and even with such simple accoutre-ments as these we see national variations on the European mainland.

In some periods the indices of importation of pottery are not known and are perhaps non-existent. However, a new form of petrological examination of wares is already throwing some light on this problem and has shown that some Dark Age imports were made in France. One must assume some direct importations by founder settlers during the major movements of people into these islands. We know of considerable trading to England during the late Neolithic to middle Bronze Age times in items other than true ceramics, such as stone, amber and gold vessels of pottery form from as far afield as Mycenae, but ceramic vessels from this source do not appear to have been found in England, although known as far as the north of Germany.

From the Belgic period of around 100 BC there was a steady flow of imported wares from northern Gaul, northern Italy, and the Mediterranean. The Roman era opened the floodgates of importation. Although it is unremarkable that the ubiquitous Samian ware from France, its close relative Arretine ware from northern Italy, amphorae, green glazed wares from St Remy and the products of the Rhenish potteries have been readily recognised, there must be other material from the wider areas of the Roman Empire still awaiting recognition.

The Roman imperial system encouraged not only inter-colonial trade but manufacture on the grand scale, and there were vast factories in Gaul which turned out quantities of Samian for export to known parts of the Empire, including England. Factories were also set up at trading points, the Rhineland manufactories for pottery, glass and iron products being a good example of this. Although this material was produced for the German mainland, much of the pottery found its way to Britain. Still other materials came as containers for oils, wines, and other liquid goods; these are known as amphorae, and are thought to have come from the countries around the Mediterranean.

In the three centuries following the departure of the Romans from England trade was continued between Greece, Spain, France and North Africa to the countries of the Celtic West, Cornwall, Wales, Ireland and Scotland. These took the form of amphorae, dishes and bowls, some with Christian motifs.

The pagan Saxons certainly brought examples of pottery with them, as some of the early examples found here mirror the products of their native heath. Some importations to Saxon England from Merovingian France took place during this period; many were flasks and bottles and perhaps held liquids of special significance.

In the late Saxon period importation from the Rhineland became a considerable business, and the rapidly developing factories at Pingsdorf, Limburg and other places produced goods widely acceptable in Western Europe and found in many parts of England. This strong trade continued into the eleventh century when the bias of importation swung towards France following the Norman Conquest, the earliest examples coming from the north and west. By the thirteenth century the bulk was coming from the south-west of France, although there was a widening focus with products coming in from the whole of the French and Dutch littoral and the Rhineland kilns. By the end of this century the spectrum had widened still, and now included the products of Turkey, Greece, Italy, Spain (in quantity), and a little from the East Mediterranean.

This importation increased throughout the post-medieval period and brought imports from all the potting centres of Western Europe both on the coast and from well inland— Spain, Portugal, northern Italy, the Mediterranean islands— also from the Near East, North Africa, Indo-China and China proper. It is the imports from China that acquired significance in the late sixteenth century and developed rapidly in the ensuing century to become the dominant import. Although German salt-glazed wares continued to be imported in increasing amounts between the seventeenth and nineteenth centuries, and Dutch delfts streamed across the Channel, the desire was for more and more porcelain, making it the most important item not just as an import, but as a major influence on our ceramic history.

Imports have at times had a considerable influence on our ceramic traditions. Of course, it was often the *idea* that was imported. The abrupt changes of the Beaker period were imported, the major influences on design and technology of the later Iron Age were imported, and so on through the obviously imported ideas of the Romans, pagan Saxon, and late Saxon material and ideas. Even as late as 1671 the art of making salt-glazed stonewares had to be imported from Germany. The importation of actual vessels also had an influence on native products. The Belgae copied *terra nigra*, the native Britains copied first-century Roman wares, and the late Roman potters in East Anglia copied the wares of the incoming Saxons. The tenth-century ceramic renaissance produced copies of wares made in the Rhineland. In the Middle Ages French imports had some effect on the English wares, and some local forms were strongly influenced in this way. In the immediate post-medieval period the influence of French wares is noticeable, especially on some high-quality wares, and it now seems likely that the famed Cistercian wares were influenced directly from the Low Countries; slipwares are now known to have had their origins there. Delftware which was to become so abundant in the seventeenth and eighteenth centuries was an imported industry from Holland. The ubiquitous porcelain of Chinese origin was first successfully copied in Italy, from which source the idea was brought to England in the middle of the eighteenth century. The last source of imports to affect ceramics on the grand scale were those classical curios, relics of the 'Grand Tour', which became the principal influences on Wedgwood and Bentley.

The influence and exchanges of imports do not cease, and we see the results today of the Anglo-Nipponese school, fostered by Leach, and continued, already modified, by his followers.

There is perhaps only one occasion on which English potters have developed a new idea that is of importance—the development of the medieval jug. By the end of the thirteenth century and through the fourteenth such vessels were common over Western Europe from Scandinavia to northern Italy. On the Continent they appear over a short period of time as fully developed and highly decorated vessels without the precursors common to any medium with a natural development, whereas in England we can see the jug growing out of a series of forms until its shape becomes established by the early twelfth century.

Pottery made in England was exported. For the periods before the advent of Rome in England we have no information, but it is thought that some of the products of the vast Nene Valley manufactories were sent to northern France and the German *Limes*. It is not until the Middle Ages that we have strong evidence of the export of ceramics to Scandinavia and northern Germany. In the sixteenth century, with the foundation of the American colonies and the Indian and Baltic trading companies, the export of home-produced wares increased. Export continued to spread to British India, Australia, New Zealand and the Pacific islands from the end of the

age 51 (*right*) Late Neolithic/
:arly Bronze Age beaker.
)ecorated with impressed cord
nd a 'rims and dot' motif
1ade with the cut end of a
ollow bone. From Lang-
ourne Down, Berkshire.
below) Bronze Age food
essels. Small versions of the
.rge burial urns. (*left*) coarse
ecorated with applied pieces.
rom Good Manham, York-
iire; (*right*) heavily decorated
ith impressed cord patterns.
rom Sherborne, Yorkshire

Page 52 (*above*) Bronze Age incense cups. A group of five showing the wide variety of form and decoration met with in these vessels; (*upper left*) unprovenenced; (*upper right*) Cliffe Hill, Lewes, Sussex; (*lower left*) Bulford, Wiltshire; (*lower right*) Roughridge Hill, Wiltshire. (*left*) Bronze Age bucket urn. Coarse decorated vessel with an inward sloping neck and two small projecting lings. Lambourne Barrows, Berkshire.

eighteenth century, and became the life-blood of the trade during the latter part of the nineteenth century and up to today. Even large sections of nineteenth-century New York were built with bricks made for that end in the Buckley Brick Works in North Wales.

Chapter Two

The Ceramic Development

This chapter deals with the currently accepted ceramic types illustrative of each particular period. This will preclude a wide number of variations, as throughout the history of ceramics such variations occur in each region no matter how sophisticated or unsophisticated their period. Each potter adds to or subtracts from a design to his own liking, or to his own ability, and although quality is an important factor, individual ability should not reflect on the whole, and the whole for each region is often strikingly different from that of its neighbour.

These developments are listed according to the accepted archaeological periods, which are:

Neolithic (early and middle)	(—) 3500 BC to (+)	2000 BC
Late Neolithic to early Bronze Age	2000 BC to	1500 BC
Bronze Age	1500 BC to	600 BC
Iron Age (Hallstatt, La Tène, Belgic)	(—) 600 BC to (+)	AD 43
Romano-British	AD43 to	AD 450
Dark Ages (Celtic West and pagan Saxon)	(—) AD 400 to	AD 700
Middle and late Saxon	AD 700 to	AD 1000
Saxo-Norman	AD 1000 to	AD 1150
Medieval	AD 1150 to	AD 1450
Post-medieval	AD 1450 to	AD 1750
Industrial	AD 1750 –	

Such a date range as offered here is currently accepted, but as it is liable to review it should be treated only as a general guide.

The Neolithic Period

The New Stone Age (Neolithic) saw the foundations of civilisations, groups of human beings gathering together in one place permanently for the first time. Such settlement demanded an agricultural basis and it occurred in areas in which staple cereal crops grew, and in which either adequate game reserves were available or the sheep and goat which were man's domesticated types could be kept. By this time certain of the handcrafts normal to advanced primitive communities were well developed. The communities rapidly developed the skills requisite to urban life, inasmuch as they learned about drainage and water supply, about house, storehouse and temple building and the construction and management of streets, squares, markets, as well as the building of substantial defences such as great ditches, thick, high walls and massive towers.

The sedentary nature of urban life allows for some time to be devoted to subjects other than the mundane, and for thought to be applied to solution and invention. But even so, it was some considerable time before pottery was invented, as the great city of Jericho shows that its early layers were constructed by non-pottery-using people. It is thought that the manufacture of pottery in the western hemisphere was developed somewhere in what is now Turkey about 7000 BC. Once the skill was fully mastered and the products appreciated, their use spread throughout the Fertile Crescent, which stretches from Syria round to Pakistan. Pottery then came into common use amongst all the Neolithic communities of the Middle East. The culture of these urban communities then spread, either by actual movements of comprehending settlers or by indirect influence on local people. As these influences were mobile the greater skills of building, fortification etc were not so readily carried, and only those of a slighter nature such as the growing of crops, tending of flocks, advanced handcrafts including potting, and finally religion were more readily dispersed. This spread, as far as England is concerned, came from the Middle East along the southern Mediterranean littoral, across into Spain and France, then via the narrows of the English Channel to the Chalk Downs of England. This early Neolithic culture has its influence on the indigenous populations which were in the Middle Stone Age (Mesolithic) stage of development and are thought to have had no knowledge of pottery-making. This indigenous population probably continued as a separate culture for a long time, absorbing new ideas and eventually making pottery of its own. The pottery of the Neolithic period can be divided into Early, Middle and Late classes.

EARLY TO MIDDLE NEOLITHIC

Fabric Coarse with some fine tempering
Method of Manufacture Hand-made
Firing Oxidising clamps
Principal characteristics Complete or lower portions of vessels hemispherical. Some decoration increasing towards the end of the phase

The earliest forms are thought to be those recognised at Windmill Hill, Avebury, Wiltshire. These are well made with a smooth and often burnished surface. They are bag-shaped and have a plain rim or are set above a wide groove and slightly turned out. Many examples have solid lugs projecting at either side of the vessel; in some examples these are hollow. Both types are thought to be aids for the suspension of the vessel. Windmill Hill pottery is lightly decorated, and such decoration as does occur is of two types, namely 'burnishing' and 'grooving'. A vessel is burnished when it is 'leather' hard, when the surface can be polished by being abraded with a hard, smooth object such as a pebble, a piece of wood or a rib bone. When fired this shine is retained. Burnishing sometimes alters the surface tension causing post-firing flaking. Grooving is the name given to one of the commonest forms of pottery decoration, by incising the surface of the vessel when either wet or dry. In general, grooves incised on the outside of pottery appear to be made with the rounded end of a stick or rod. These grooves throughout the history of English potting are in the main between 2mm and 4mm in thickness.

Strongly associated with the Windmill Hill tradition and thought to mark a stage of development is that known from the type site of Peterborough. Here the ware is round-based with coarse and thick walls. They generally have a well-defined rim above a deep neck groove, a feature of all the vessels of this form. Ornamentation is profuse, using 'whipped cord', 'finger-tipping', 'stamping' and 'combing and grooving'. Whipped cord decoration is of some importance as it is long-lived and goes through to the end of the Bronze Age. This singular decorative motif was achieved simply by impressing string on to the wet body of the pot in a variety of ways, leaving a unique and unmistakable impression. Fingertipping is the term used to describe a method of making small dish-shaped depressions set inside a slight ridge by impressing the wet surface of the vessel with the tip of the finger. A developed form of this is achieved by forming precise dished indentations by using the broad of the thumb; these indentations occur round the shoulder of the vessel. Stamping of the body while wet is a process met with increasingly during this period. This takes the form of patterns or single random applications. In this case the stamps may be cuneiform, or the articular ends of the bones of small birds and less frequently of small mammals. Similar use was made of the rippled edge of the cardium shell, a product of the sea-shore and therefore transported inland for this or some other specific purpose. Combing is another form of decoration very common to most of the periods of this history. It is achieved very simply be passing the teeth of a comb or rake-shaped tool over the surface of a wet or leather-state vessel in either vertical, horizontal, angular or most commonly in wavy patterns. On Peterborough vessels chevron combing and/or grooving occurs on the neck groove and down the body of the vessel.

The influence of this second phase of early Neolithic appears

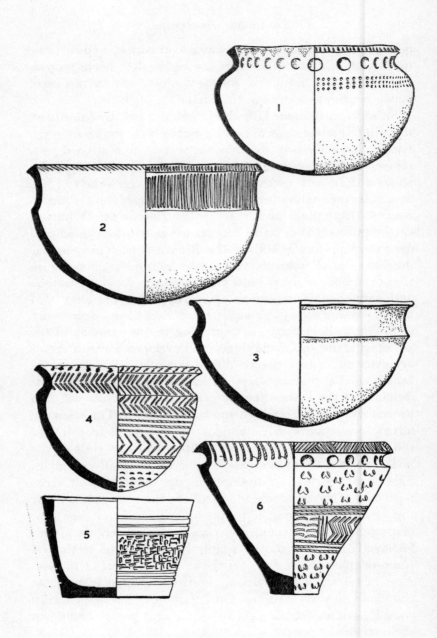

to have spread throughout the whole of the east of Britain, from the English Channel to the Firth of Forth, with the principal concentration in the Thames Valley, and it is relatively unknown in the western half of England. There are cultural affinities to this phase, and sub-species are known at various sites. At Hembury, Devon, the forms comprise long, bag-shaped pots and open bowls with lugs that are either solid or in the form of bell-ended tubes. This type is undecorated. From Abingdon, Berkshire, there are similar baggy forms with thickened rims and lug handles, although in this instance strap handles occur—flat strips of clay coiled into loops. Abingdon ware is profusely decorated. Similar examples also come from Whitehawk, Sussex, and East Anglia, but these are considered to belong to a later stage of this phase.

One feature unique to this early phase of Neolithic potting and unique to the whole history of English ceramics is the production of a 'spoon'. These are about 22cm long, hand-made from a solid piece of clay, square in section and tapering like a blunt peg at one end and dished out in oval or egg-shaped form at the other. The purpose of these is not understood. Their construction and quality, which are generally poor, would appear to preclude domestic use. They are found casually and not in burial mounds of the period, in France and in England only in association with Windmill Hill culture sites.

MID TO LATE NEOLITHIC

Fabric Very coarse
Method of Manufacture Hand-made
Firing Uncontrolled oxidising clamps with a tendency to reduce
Principal characteristics Forms similar to early Neolithic but with an admixture of flat and hemispherical bases with a tendency towards all flat bases at the end of the period. Most heavily decorated

---

1–6 Neolithic types—decorations
Shallow indentations (1, 6) Small round indentations (1) Rough grooving (5) Fine grooving (1, 2, 6) Impressed cord (4, 6) Bird-bone impressions (6) 'Cardium shell' impressions (6)

The end of the first phase of the Neolithic potting tradition is marked by the end of regional style and its replacement by a general uniformity of style and form; this new type is known as Ebbsfleet ware from the site where it was first recognised.

By this time the pottery has become cruder, coarser in texture, poorer in finish, and very heavily decorated. The forms parallel those of the early Neolithic (also known to archaeologists as 'Western Neolithic') in many respects, but there is an increasing use of flat bases, which were first seen during the 'Peterborough' era. Flat bases continue to spread in use until the Neolithic round-based vessel disappears altogether. The flatbased vessels, once established, increase in size and lay the foundations for the early forms of the ensuing Bronze Age.

A notable feature of the potting of this phase is the use of 'grog' as a tempering medium. Grog is the term applied to small fragments of crushed pottery being used in place of other opening material in the fabric, in addition to, or instead of the other normal tempering agents.

The Ebbsfleet types are standard, round-bottomed, grooved and shouldered bowls, some of which have simple plain rims like early Neolithic types, but others have elaborate T-sectioned inturned rim forms. They also have deep indentations round the shoulders. Secondary to the Ebbsfleet style is a form known from Mortlake, which is coarser, larger and ornamented over the whole of the surface. Both these wares in the upper part of their date range have characteristics borrowed from Beakers, showing how they continue into the late Neolithic. The last phase of true Neolithic pottery was that named after Fengate. Such vessels are predominantly flat-based and bucketshaped, and although some still have a pronounced groove under the rim and indentations round the collar, in some instances the upper portion of the rim has been projected slightly and the collar groove done away with. Fingertipping and a form of finger-nail impression are found as well as frequent use of cord impressions. By the time these wares were in common use the Bronze Age was already well established in the south of England.

OTHER EXAMPLES OF NEOLITHIC WARES

The spread of this culture's pottery to the outer areas is important. The spread was northwards and westwards, and there are several important type sites which show this movement to advantage. In Grimston, Yorkshire, the bag-shaped pottery is well made and has a pronounced S-shaped profile, in which the bowls are heightened and have an outward-turning shoulder piece. Here, they are undecorated. In the Severn Valley the forms are simple and the body has an admixture of shell as a tempering medium. In the Clyde Valley there are two main groups, one of which is well made and bears decoration limited to burnishing and rippling of the surface of the body while wet. The other group is coarser and known from the type site as Beacharra ware; this is long-lived and has three stages of development. The first phase produced simple, bag-shaped pots with lugs which were undecorated, the second phase was decorated with deep grooves, and the final phase was decorated with whipped cord. In the north of Ireland around the valley of the Boyne the pottery is very coarse and is heavily tempered with quartzite. These vessels appear to have been coil-built; they are of simple form, mainly open bowls with heavy rims, and are decorated with coarse grooving and heavy combing. Further north in the Hebrides the forms range from bag-shaped to pointed-base forms, the shoulders are slight, and lugs are infrequent. In the Orkneys the styles are simple and the decoration limited to simple grooves or fingertipping, or else extremely complex, depending on the time factor. Heavy decoration on crude vessels is made in zones which are filled with a variety of media such as impressed whipped cord, bird and small mammal bone-end stamps, deep grooving and cross-hatching grooves. In some the zones are roughed by the wet clay being lifted by suction on the ball of the finger and then allowed to dry. This process is known as rustication. Some of these vessels have holes pierced through their upper parts for suspension. Some other examples have 'applied strip' decoration. This is the application of a strip of clay to the vessel, and it is used in a wide and complex form throughout the history of English potting. In this instance the method is used in a striking fashion as relief moulding, in which the pieces are applied to both the inside and the outside of the vessel in abstract linear designs which are subsequently embellished with light hatching. In the Isle of Man at Ronalsway, there are large jars up to 37cm high and 20cm across which are of truly situlate (bucket) shape, as well as small cups with flat bases.

The Neolithic cultures as we see them here in the space of a few pages took a considerable time to develop and to spread throughout the length and breadth of this long island. It is for this reason that, as I stated at the beginning of this book, this history is confined to England. In the history of English potting there can be no more important phase than the foundation of the industry. The Neolithic is not only the longest single phase of development, but one which set the seal on a stage of development which was to continue for a considerable period. In the 2,000 years between the first landing of potmakers somewhere on the Sussex coast to the last of the Neolithic in islands of the north, the difficult skill of making a pot was learnt, dispersed, understood and elaborated, so that by the time new things were beginning about 2000 BC an English style had developed, within the framework of a new society.

The Late Neolithic Period and the Bronze Age

This period is marked by the incidence of bronze usage. Of equal and perhaps complementary importance is the consolidation of the Neolithic socio-religious structure readily apparent in the construction of extant monuments of considerable size such as Silbury Hill, Avebury circle and the early Stonehenge with its stones imported from Wales. Sight should not be lost of the period's achievements, even in the lesser realms of large burial mounds, standing timber 'temples', and the mining, manufacture and trading of stone axes. Ceramically the story is relatively simple, set against the backcloth of great things, for it does in a simple and steadfast way reflect the slow evolution of the culture, its economic, social and religious conditions that prevailed in the 1,400 years of its tenure.

LATE NEOLITHIC AND BEAKER PERIOD

Fabric Very fine with grog tempering
Method of manufacture Hand-made, some certainly coil-built, others including some cylindrical beakers could have been made by slabbing
Firing The finer wares certainly used some form of controlled oxidising clamp
Principal characteristics Late Neolithic: situlate urns with slightly overhanging rims. Beaker: drinking vessel of about quartern capacity; some are cylindrical with handles, others have globular lower halves and straight necks, others flaring necks, profusely decorated.

Coming as it were between the Neolithic ceramic amalgam and the subsequent full flowering of the native Bronze Age there is a vigorous and dominating invasion of an advanced stage of the Neolithic culture by the Beaker people, by which the period is known. It is the only period in English history to which a ceramic name is given. These people brought with them not only the knowledge of bronze usage, gold ornamentation, and single burial, all apparently within the same social and religious tenure, but a new vessel, a large, handle-less drinking cup, a beaker. These vessels, though unique in form and technically highly developed, can be seen from their decoration to be within the sphere of Neolithic ceramic culture. They became general throughout England but occur mainly in Wessex, that vast chalkland that lies to the north of the Hampshire basin, and also in the south-east of England.

Beakers are very well made in relation to the bulk of the then current native wares, although there was also a marked improvement in many areas. The fabric of beakers is very fine indeed and such tempering as can be seen is either of a very fine sand or well-ground grog. The use of grog in this context and in the other current Neolithic wares is the first recorded instance of the practice of pre-fired (and therefore pre-shrunk) tempering agents being included, a practice that seems to have ended with the early Bronze Age vessels and not to have been

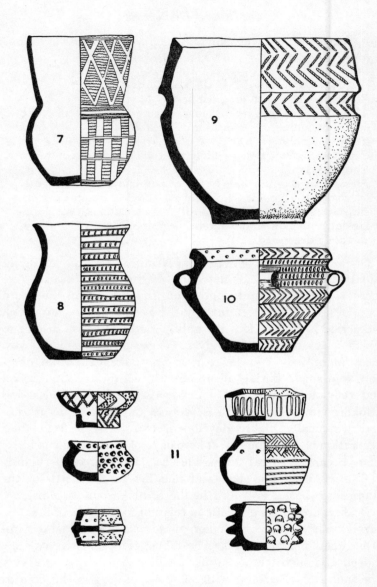

introduced into this country again until the eighteenth century.

Another dominant feature in the techniques of producing this group of wares is that they are oxidised, usually to a shade of buff that is recognisably standard over wide geographical areas and for relatively long periods of time. These two factors argue for some special technique in the firing processes. Again, in this as in other periods there were areas where this process was not practised or understood, and there was a tendency to reduction, coarse fabrics and clumsy workmanship, although such wares are in the minority.

Beakers are classified into three groups: Bi, Bii, and A, so enumerated because the initial classification has been altered as the result of recent study. These identifications are given to shapes: Bi is globular with a short, wide neck, Bii has a globular lower half with a vase-shaped neck and rim, and A has a globular base with a short neck and rim. They stand between 20cm and 30cm high. They are profusely decorated in a variety of forms. The main types of decoration are zonal and horizontal lines determining the zones, each alternating zone being filled with a wide variety of grooved motifs. In some instances the grooves are burnished. Whipped cord decoration is very common, some beakers being entirely decorated by having a whipped cord carefully wrapped round the whole exterior of the vessel, and as these show no sign of disturbance the cord was probably left to burn away in the fire.

Such vessels are fairly common in the areas in which they are found. They formed a part of the domestic scene and are also found as casual fragments. The bulk, however, come from

---

7–11   Early Bronze Age types
7–8   Beakers decorated with impressed cord (7) and grooving (8) (9)   Overhanging rim urn decorated with impressed cord (10) 'Food vessel' decorated with grooving and piercing on the rim (11)   A selection of 'cups' of ritual significance decorated in traditional patterns of the period, including large round balls attached to the outside of the vessel, as in the example at the bottom of the row. These are known as 'grape cups'

burial groups and formed an important part of the last rites. In this instance Beakers cannot be considered as funerary vessels in their own right as are vessels in other periods, but they are important in this particular aspect as they, or at least their owners, set off a long chain of similar events which continued through a large portion of our ceramic history. It is worthy of note that some of those found in association with the dead do have a special quality that is superior to the wares of more common use.

The Beaker period was more than an anomaly; it was a catalyst that converted and modified the existing culture, and ceramically it set standards of quality that were to have an effect on the contemporary wares and on the early stages of decoration of the wares of the next period.

The closing stages of the Neolithic period are marked by two stages of development, the continuation of the by-now native product and a secondary individual vessel growing out of the demands of the Beaker cultures. The terminal native forms are known from their type site of Fengate, as described above, and we see that these have gone on well into the Bronze Age but in use as domestic vessels by now to be known as situlate urns derived from a late form of Neolithic wares known as Mortlake type and influenced strongly by both Beaker decoration, manufacturing techniques and burial customs. These vessels are large and can be 25cm high by 15cm wide at the rim, and as they are found solely in round barrows derived from Beaker traditions containing cremated remains of humans they are thought to have been made specifically for that purpose. Such vessels are flat-based with a dished lower portion above which is the groove that had been included as a standard feature on every vessel since the beginning of the Neolithic. This factor of illustrating a cultural mark at a point about three-quarters of the way up the side of a vessel is of note, for in this instance this point of marking has a long period of usage. Starting with a groove in the earliest of Neolithic vessels, it continued as a groove until the middle of the Bronze Age, when it very gradually obtained a dominating upper overhanging edge; this in its turn became a heavy flange which over a considerable period of time gradually came down to being an applied cordon, and this in its turn finally terminated in a decoration of finger-tipping before both the decoration and the pot types vanished. This use of this zone on the vessels for decoration must have some significance, for it began in 3500 BC and continued through the Bronze Age, ending some time after 300 BC.

Above the groove these collared urns, as they are called, have an inward sloping collar with a plain rim. These vessels appear to be tempered only with grog. Although they are related to Beakers in this respect and in the use of profuse Beaker ornamentation, they are altogether inferior in manufacture, and although there are in the early phases of the Bronze Age other vessels which do uphold the fine potting tradition of the Beakers, there is always that measure of incompetence which is quite sharply marked in varying regions and different styles as if ability ebbed and flowed according to the demands of culture and religion. The collared urn was the foundation vessel of a long series and was itself long-lived, being thought to have been produced for some 500 years at least.

EARLY BRONZE AGE

Fabrics Of a wide variety of types ranging in quality from that equal to Beakers to the coarsest, depending upon the area from which they come

Method of manufacture Hand-made, some suggestion of coil-building

Firing Some controlled oxidising clamps, many uncontrolled clamps giving a variety of finishes

Principal characteristics The development of the situlate vessel with a pronounced rim as seen in the final stages of the late Neolithic. The production of a wide variety of small funerary accessory vessels. Much decoration in the beginning, becoming less at the end

Allied to collared urns, Beakers and Fengate pots, these 'food vessels', as they are called, are the outcome of a terminal amalgam of all these sundry sub-strata vessels. Once again they appear to be primarily funerary in character. The graves in which they are discovered also quite often contain the small funerary vessels known as incense cups. These incense cups, common to the Wessex end of the early parts of this culture, are a varied form of small vessel varying from 6cm to 10cm wide by 2cm high. Although known simply as cups, some are also known as Aldbourne cups, pigmy cups or grape cups. The latter vessels are covered all over the outside with a rash of small, regular, applied balls of clay; between each lump a thin hole has been pierced through. The incense cups are made with plain side walls in which holes or slots have been cut. Some of these cups are merely carefully made miniatures of the larger funerary satulate vessels. Many are further embellished with whipped cord, grooving or rusticated decoration. Such vessels, however, were obviously infrequently produced and their variety in a minor degree is considerable. There is also ceramic quality in the workmanship of some examples which is far superior to the contempory larger vessels.

Food vessels developed in those areas strong in the late Neolithic cultural traditions, and in England the North Riding of Yorkshire and Wessex predominated, although there are noticeable groups in the Midlands, in the Peak District, and in Scotland in the south-east and through the Lowlands. The ceramic forms from north of a line Dublin–Galway are among the finest examples. These vessels, similar to the corded urns, stand about 30cm high and are about 23cm across the mouth, tapering to a flat base. In these we see a continuation of the general development from the late Neolithic, but with the development to one, two or even three grooves round the neck and with well-developed strong rim forms, often with wide flanges on the inside cocked at an angle for the display of elaborate incised decoration. In many examples the grooves are filled in at regular interval with 'stops'. Each stop is then pierced with a fine hole. In some cases the groove is not filled in but is bridged over by a strap handle which forms a tube. Both the pierced stops and the tubes suggest that these vessels were suspended at some time. Towards the end of this primary phase new forms of collared urn appear which stand up to 35cm

Page 69 (above) Iron Age situla and 'omphalos' base bowl. Two vessels found together in the same deposit. Linford Quarry, Mucking, Essex. (*right*) Iron Age jar decorated with abstract curvilinear designs in a band around the shoulder. Meare Lake village, Somerset

Page 70 (*above*) Romano-British lead glazed wares. First and second century. (*upper right*) an imported flagon found at Colchester; (*upper middle* and *left*) from Jordan Hill; (*lower left*) from Colchester; (*right*) from Ewell, Surrey. (*below*) Romano-British Nene Valley ware. Three examples of wares made in the extensive factories in this region; (*left*) black slip with white slip over; (*middle and right*) coated with a metallic slip giving a bronzed finish.

high; these vessels are bucket-shaped with a marked inward-sloping bold shoulder to a well-made, flat, squared rim.

In its early stages the pottery of this phase is frequently of good quality. The underlying native Neolithic tradition is still constant but poorer quality of workmanship begins to sap the strength of the better material and there is a gradual decline in fabric, firing and decoration. At the end of the phase the miniature vessels, which were predominantly of grape-cup form in the beginning, have become flat-based and cylindrical-bodied with a pronounced flaring rim. These vessels are decorated with geometric designs made by grooving or with whipped cord. Many of these vessels are also pierced or slotted in some way. Finally there is a series of vessels found in fairly large numbers in graves of this period which are mostly on the small side by comparison with the standard type and range from highly decorated to plain, their shapes varying from barrel or tumbler form to exact miniatures of the principal vessels.

MIDDLE TO LATE BRONZE AGE

Fabric Wide variety of qualities, ranging from coarse to very coarse

Method of manufacture Hand-made with a possibility of coil-building predominating

Firing Uncontrolled clamps producing a variety of finishes

Principal characteristics The establishment of large, situlate burial urns; these are sometimes associated with a secondary vessel in the early stages of the period. Decoration gradually decreases until in some areas it disappears altogether

By the middle Bronze Age there is a general reduction of types to one principal form of vessel and to some varying secondary vessels. The funerary urns large enough to take the unbroken cremated long bones of a fully mature adult dominate the field, and they become the primary product. These vessels are also made for domestic use and we see them beginning to be found at the few settlement sites of this period that are so far known. By this phase it would seem that the major portion of the product was manufactured for funerary purposes, or per-

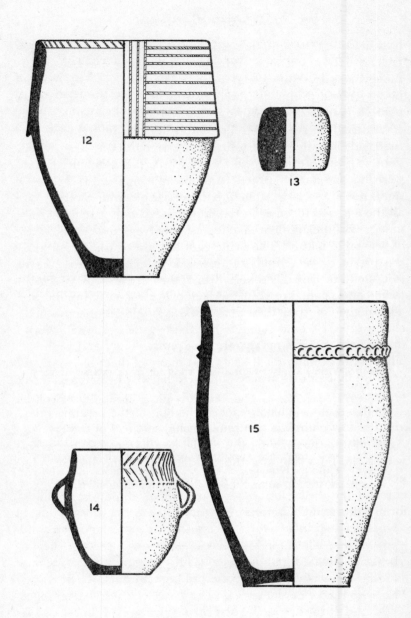

haps it is just that the domestic habits of the Bronze Age are not yet fully understood. Whatever the reason, the quality of these vessels is very poor and it can be stated unequivocally that pottery made during the last phase of the Bronze Age is the poorest manufactured during the whole history of English ceramics. The vessels were probably all coil-built in fabrics that had only the most rudimentary preparation. The inclusions vary according to the source of the fabric material and were not carefully selected; they include fine sands, gravels, small stones and large stones up to the size of a pullet's egg, and all these mixed together in the same pot. Also, it is not uncommon to find the unintentional inclusion of twigs and other pieces of vegetable matter. The firing is of the most casual form and the products as a result of this lack of expertise are rarely suitable to be called ceramics, which they are only by virtue of their conversion rate being well above the 500°C minimum. The method of firing these vessels was certainly in uncontrolled clamps and I would suggest that those vessels especially produced for a given funeral were fired individually and rapidly. This would account for the fact that many of them have only a very lightly oxidised surface and are otherwise heavily reduced inside.

At this point we have reached the ebb of the ceramic tide, and this low point will continue through the end of the Bronze Age and into the early part of the Hallstatt Iron Age, but even within the final stages of the middle part of the Bronze Age newly introduced improved types are already becoming apparent and there develops a separate school of potters making forms not met with before.

12–15   Late Bronze Age types
12   Collared urn, decorated with cord impressions.
13   Cylindrical loom-weight, used to weight the warp on an upright loom.
14   Globular urn, decorated with grooving and piercing.
15   Bucket urn with applied strip and finger-dimpling. A transitional type.

A prime type of vessel which in the south-east of England is considered as the ultimate native development is known as the bucket urn. In this the collared urn has lost its groove and its overhanging decorated rim and has become reduced to a bi-conical vessel, the groove still apparent on some and even an attempt at retaining the rim on others, but these features on most having been replaced by a thumbed applied strip, or just a single row of widely spaced thumbed jabs into the fabric of the vessel. Twisted cord is still in fairly common use but in a ragged and irregular fashion. Many have opposing lugs mounted at the shoulder; some of these are pierced through either vertically or horizontally. Applied pieces in the forms of in-verted horseshoes heavily fingerprinted occur commonly on some localised vessels in Wessex. Many other types have in-turned or flanged small rims which are frequently decorated either with twisted cord or with fingertipping. Bucket urns fall into the poor-quality group of products. They were obvi-ously fired in uncontrolled reducing conditions, resulting in colour shades of dark iron to black. They are tall vessels, ranging from about 25cm to 60cm; the wide mouths can measure the same as the height of the vessel or slightly less. Although the quality of these vessels is undeniably poor, there are again variations and some excellently produced examples are known.

Two other forms of vessel appear in the Wessex area about this time, barrel urns and globular urns. Both differ from the local product and demonstrate a higher standard of skill than those of the native-derived type. The quality of the wares is often equal to that of food vessels. The fabric is made up from roasted and crushed flint or other fine material and in chalky or limestone-rich areas these materials are added to the temper-ing agents; in other areas shell may be added. The tendency is for globular urns to be of better quality than the rest. The barrel urns vary in size along the same lines as those of the bucket urns. They have a convex body, and they may have a double bevelled rim and be heavily corded in the form of applied strips decorated with fingertipping. They can also be utterly plain, and it is only their shape and quality that divides them from the more common and much longer lived bucket urns. Globular urns, on the other hand, are of a form that is new to our vocabulary of vessels. Coarser than barrel urns, they have a very wide distribution, and are the dominant vessel representing the Bronze Age in some areas where barrow burials are not common, for this late form of vessel is also found in 'urnfields' —an advanced stage of funerary disposal which comprises flat and by now unmarked burial areas where the system of cremation and burial of the ashes in an urn continues but with the urns placed together in a cemetery. Such changes in burial habits and other more significant features mark the beginning of the end of the Bronze Age and the subsequent special manufacture of funerary vessels.

The globular forms are principally of an S-shaped profile with a wide, rotund lower portion and a constricted collar above it. At the junction of the body and the collar there are on some varieties small pierced lugs somewhat after the fashion of those seen on the bucket urns. The surface of these vessels is often burnished and the whole of the decorative technique in many cases appears to have been undertaken after the vessel had been dried out to leather state, as the dominant motif is the groove which in this instance and because of the hard condition of the vessel is often very shallow. The grooves are in a variety of patterns in which horizontal lines, chevrons, deltas and wavy lines play a part. This group is thought to have spread eastwards from the Cornish peninsula.

The sequence of occurrence in the dating of these groups appears to be that barrel and globular urns were contemporary and were gradually superseded by the bucket urn which was to become the main form of vessel in the Iron Age that followed. These three groups of vessels are only those types that can be readily illustrated as belonging to the end of the Bronze Age. Other sub-types such as the biconical, sub-biconical and sub-bucket urns etc, as they are variously described, only go to illustrate just how much in the melting pot is the fate of English ceramics between the years *c*900 to *c*600 BC.

One feature that appeared in the late Bronze Age and was a product of this change is the ceramic loom-weight. These are cylindrical, of about 15cm long by 7cm wide, pierced through the length with a hole up to 1cm across. Such weights are indicative of settlement and of the use of domestic looms. Being late Bronze Age in date, they do in some cases overlap into the Iron Age which also had a loom-weight of distinctive form. The Bronze Age weights were made from the same coarse material as the vessels and indeed often of coarser material. They were fired in open-clamp conditions and usually have a soft, oxidised surface and a dark grey harder interior.

The Bronze Age drew to a close through a series of increased interference by settling groups from the Continent, and to some extent under the influence of traded goods and cultures from the same source. The biggest change of all was to come in the change of religion. That of the Bronze Age, great and powerful enough to raise the monument of Stonehenge and similar structures, was already in decline with the onset of new cultures carried by warlike iron-using settlers.

The Iron Ages

So called for the introduction of iron for use as tools, agricultural implements and above all for weapons, this is a period of considerable change, in industry, trade, and communications, and particularly in art, coinage and method of warfare, and in the Druidical religion. As far as this book is concerned, the ceramic changes are dramatic and memorable. This culture, as it was seen in England, had its origins in the fastnesses of the Austrian Alps whence it spread across France where it became the entrenched universal cultural occupation by the time of Caesar. Gaul was so called after the Latin name for the Celtic totem, the cock (*Gallus gallus*), and it is the Iron Age peoples who brought the Celtic languages and religions there. By their close association with the more advanced cultures of the Mediterranean, their traditions and material culture were influenced from these sources and yet in the first stages were not wholly removed from their Bronze Age traditions. This period is generally divided into three parts, named from the type-sites: Iron-Age 'A' (Hallstatt, the Austrian type-site), Iron Age 'B' (La Tène, the Swiss type-site), Iron-Age 'C', (Belgic, the name of the tribal area of northern France from which these people originated). There are many, many divisions and sub-divisions of the Iron Age period which is confused by the continuance of settlement of either A or B people for long periods, while other fairly rapid inter-cultural changes were going on, often in close proximity to these areas. The absorption of new ideas in ceramic forms and manufacturing traditions also took place very slowly in some areas, whilst in others the change was dramatic and yet in others the gelling of these confused ideas brought out striking new ideas, showing a greater advance of ceramic technology in this period than in the preceding 3,000 years.

IRON AGE 'A' (HALLSTATT)

Fabric Still very coarse but with some general improvement, especially towards the end of the period. Tempering with unselected media or with a very fine tempering fill which appears almost negligible
Method of manufacture Hand-made. The situlae probably coil-built, the bowls by the lump method
Firing In the early stages casually, as with some of the Bronze Age vessels, but later marked improvements in quality indicate controlled clamp-firing
Principal characteristics Two forms of vessel, the situlate jar and the small bowl. Decoration on the situlate commencing with simple thumbing and grooving which becomes more developed. The use of a colour coating. At the end of the phase the reintroduction of stamped ornamentation

The vessels of this period comprise two forms, a large urn and a small bowl. These vessels are not just different in size but frequently different in quality. The urns are on average 45cm high, they are made in a three-part form with the lower two-thirds in a steeply angled bucket shape, the upper portion or shoulder inclining inwards and the whole surmounted by an upright collared rim. The incidence of the line of break coming in the profile of the vessel at about the same place as that seen on vessels in the preceding periods is worth noting as a further indication of the continuance of tradition right through into this phase. The shape of these urns copies, or is copied by, bronze buckets of the period; they are known therefore as bucket urns or situlae. The quality of the wares varies enormously from site to site, but in general the quality improves throughout the phase beginning with wares made with coarse and relatively unselected tempering media which were fired obviously in the same tradition as was to be seen in some of the poorer wares of the late Bronze Age. The improvement is marked by a gradual change to thinner walled vessels with a medium that can appear to be selected, sorted or riddled to a size, or a fabric more carefully prepared. In this later development it is common to see wares that are fully oxidised—that is, they are, if made from an iron-bearing clay, red in colour. This is the first occasion on which we have seen true full oxidisation on this scale, and it is indicative either of new development or of imported ideas. The latter would seem to be the most likely in view of what was to transpire in the next phase.

The form of these vessels beginning out of late Bronze Age types with imported influences became the sharp-shouldered situlae of the high phase of the Hallstatt period. Somewhere about the middle of that phase the decline to another type of vessel began its long journey for, as in all things, the shape of pots is ever changing. The vessels gradually became smaller, the sharp profiles rounded and the lower portions globular, the upright collar also shrank in size, became rod-sectioned and lay close to the rim of the by now half-sized rounded vessel, so that at the end of the 'A' phase we have a large bead-rimmed, or, as they are sometimes called, rolled-rim vessel roughly vase-shaped in profile.

The situlate urns are not the only ceramic product of this period. There remain bowls and loom-weights. The bowls are in marked contrast to the urns, being in a very lightly tempered fabric. The method of manufacture would seem to be entirely out of the lump, by the 'hand and bat' method. They are carefully executed, and are decorated with lateral grooving within the deep groove that lies below the rim. The surface of these vessels is highly burnished and may have had haematite applied, a decorative motif that will be described in some detail below. The whole effect of these vessels is in marked contrast to the situlae that they may be found with, as they illustrate a high degree of skill. They arrived as a developed form in a spontaneous manner, indicating the new cultural milieu. The fineness of these wares may indicate a marketed product rather than the by-products of a home craft. Such practices are known for this period, particularly at the end when there is growing evidence in this phase for marketing from the area of the Malvern Hills and in the next period of marketing from areas in the south-west. The bowls are the forerunners of a long period of development, the major forms of which are known from several areas. They stand about 10cm high and are about 25cm across the mouth. They have a flared rim comprising a deep groove set above a sharply angled shoulder over the inward-sloping lower half. The bases are flat with an applied foot-ring, or flat with a dimple pressed up into the base. These characteristics, the sharp shoulder (called a carination) and the egg-shaped depression under the base (called an omphalos base), are found only on such vessels in this period.

The loom-weights met with first in the Bronze Age continued as cylindrical shapes into the first part of this period but were rapidly superseded by a form that is peculiar to this phase of the Iron Age. Indeed, it was several hundred years before the large ceramic loom-weight was to be used again. The Iron Age 'A' form is triangular, about 15cm along any length and some 5cm thick. They have holes pierced horizontally through the apex about 5cm below the point, the groups of cords being passed through two of the holes with knots tied in the third hole. In common with the Bronze Age types, the triangular weights are wholly hand-made in very poor, heavily tempered fabrics that were fired in uncontrolled clamps.

The decoration of both types of vessel was embellished by a

method used only in the Iron Age: the application of crushed haematite to the wet surface of the vessel and then burnishing that surface. When vessels that are decorated in this way are fired, the ore gives a bright red finish to them. Haematite is also known as kidney iron, a naturally and commonly occurring mineral which is found in large, knobbly lumps. When broken, it reveals a red, fan-shaped crystalline structure, and although quite hard, when crushed it produces a fine, bright red powder. This ore was also used for providing red (or black) colours in later periods, but never again simply by being added as a powder to the surface of the vessel.

The decoration of the forms of vessel not only illustrates the usual regional differences but also shows some diversification in the treatment between the two types. The decoration on the situlae commenced with the simple thumbing round the base of the neck or with simple grooving round the body. This rapidly developed to become large grooved and hatched lozenges, diamonds and triangles, and a variety of grooved zigzags. Also towards the end of this period, about the turn of the second century BC we see the emergence of stamped patterns on vessels from the Marches and West Midlands. These stamps are in what is called a 'duck' pattern, but what does emerge is a thick and shapeless 'S'. These are, however, important as the first recorded instances of purposely cut pattern stamps.

Outside our sphere of reference, in Scotland, is a group of vessels which are of typical Hallstatt form, decorated with magnificent grooved zoomorphic designs, mostly of stags. Although they occurred as late as the first century AD they too are notable as primary examples of free zoomorphic art on ceramics, native to these islands.

The bowls have strong regional characteristics. In Wessex they are plain and simple with the use of haematite prevalent. In the area of the upper Thames valley the use of haematite was limited, and both the ware and the decoration are crude. In East Anglia the bowls are heavy and larger than those in other regions. They appear to be a later introduction here than elsewhere, and rapidly developed into Iron Age 'B' types. In the

South Downs, examples have a very limited decoration and rapidly developed into bead-rimmed forms, although here the basic 'A' forms continued for longer than in most other southern counties. In the lower Thames valley there is a close affinity with the Wessex types, but the bowls get very large and emulate some of the features of the situlae. In the Chilterns the developments appear to be very late and the 'A' forms already show the influences of 'B' types on them. Going further north, types found in the valley of the Trent show a wide variety of forms consistent with their being on the periphery of the Highland zone. One feature is the 'scratch-marking' or 'grass-wiping' as it is variously called, caused by wiping the surface of the vessel while still wet with a bunch of grass.

The end of the Hallstatt period, in whatever region or at whatever date it occurs, marks the end of a distinctive and noteworthy phase in the history of English ceramic development. The hand-made pot fired in an oxidising or uncontrolled clamp kiln was the principal type produced from the introduction of the craft into this country. Following the Iron Age 'A' period we see this in decline, and it was replaced in England, to return at occasional intervals but never as the universal method of production. There is some evidence to show that in Ireland it continued in general use right up to recent historical times beyond the Pale and altered only in selected places after the Anglo-Norman invasions of the twelfth century. In Scotland the penetration was less delayed, yet in the Highlands and Islands such potting methods appear to have been practised until the nineteenth century.

IRON AGE 'B' (LA TÈNE)

Fabric In the early stages still coarse but rapidly changing to a sandy fabric as soon as the 'B' forms became established

Method of manufacture Hand-made by some refined process which produced a fine, well-finished vessel. The wheel was introduced and rapidly adopted after 100 BC

Firing The quality of the firing is equal to the rest of the potting in this phase and indicates well-controlled reducing clamps

Principal characteristics Good-quality pottery with a limited range

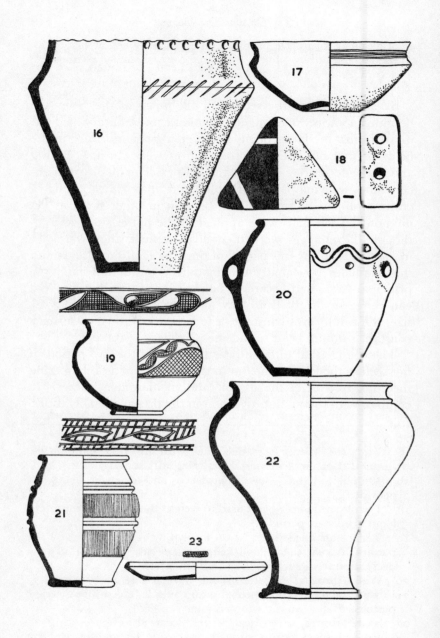

of globular forms. Decoration limited to body colour heightened by fine, all-over burnishing. In some areas inscribed linear
decoration of a very high order

By about 250 BC the second or 'B' phase of the Iron Age
heralded a variety of changes in domestic and military life, and
in art forms, the latter being of the greatest significance in the
fields of precious metals, wrought-iron work, bronze casting
and in the decoration of wood and leather. The quality of bask-
etry and weaving is remarkable, and these illustrations of
craftmanship were probably to be seen in other fields as yet
unknown. Such skills were applied to the potter's art, and although the changes were themselves radical, they were not
immediately so. By this period in time the Hallstatt situlae and
the omphalos bowl had been modified considerably and the
principal vessel had become a bowl or jar of varying size, that
can range in height from, say 45cm to 15cm. Whatever the
size, the rim form is constant, a turned-over lip which forms a
constant running bead round the periphery of the pot.

The change that differentiates the ware of the two periods is
not seen in the form alone but in the use of sand as a tempering
medium, instead of the use of random materials; there is in
compass with this an improvement in the preparation of fabrics.

16–23   Iron Age types

16   Situla (or 'bucket') urn decorated with finger-dimpling on the
rim and slashing of the shoulders (Hallstatt period).

17   'Omphalos-based' bowl, burnished and grooved (Hallstatt
period).

18   Triangular loom-weight used to weight the warp on an upright
loom (Hallstatt period).

19   'Black-burnished ware, wheel-thrown, with an incised abstract
pattern. Above and below this piece are two other examples of
decoration from such vessels (La Tène period).

20   Wheel-thrown 'black-burnished' ware (La Tène period).

21   'Butt' beaker. Wheel-turned with rouletted decoration (Belgic
period).

22   'Pedestal urn', wheel-turned (Belgic period).

23   Plate in 'black-burnished ware with potter's stamp in the form
of an ear of wheat (Belgic period).

The tempering medium is well mixed and the body is solid in its construction. What is perhaps more noteworthy is the introduction of a controlled reduction clamp which produces a totally black ware. This reduction method, as it was learned by the indigenous peoples, produced a variety of quality, but eventually totally black wares became universal, not only in this period but in related ensuing phases.

The decorations are relatively few, great store being placed on a good body colour which was further embellished by intensive burnishing, not only on the outside but also on the inside of the vessel. Added to this, there is the limited use of haematite indicating an 'A' tradition still lingering. However, the application of an abstract linear ornamentation illustrates an achievement never again surpassed in English ceramics.

Before going into the regional variations of this phase, three related items must be considered which have a bearing on the whole history of English potting. The first is the introduction of the wheel, which appears to have arrived about 100 BC. A similar date is given to the earliest invasion settlements of the Belgae, and it is to them that the wheel is attributed. Whatever the source, the highly advanced hand techniques and other skills of the Iron Age 'B' potters made them receptive of improvements, and the use of the wheel spread. This spread was not general, for the further north and west one goes from the south-east the less immediate is the impact.

The second point is that despite the introduction of the wheel and at the same time a wide variety of Belgic 'C' forms, plus the beginning of imports, the pottery forms changed very little throughout the ensuing 200 years.

The third point is that by the beginning of the Christian era, with the exception of the most outlying parts of this island, 'B' forms had come to dominate the ceramic scene and set the seal on pattern and design of many coarseware types throughout the Romano-British period.

Of importance to our story is the spread of 'B' types of similar form into the north-west of Germany where they developed slowly through the ensuing five centuries, to reappear on our shores as Saxon pots.

The regional variations are significant. In Dorset the change from 'A' types was slow and the use of haematite colouring remained but was reduced in quantity. An outstanding feature of these types is the 'countersunk' handles in which a groove is indented at each side of a vessel, over which is set a short rod-sectioned handle which matches the profile of the vessel, giving the impression of a pierced hole. These handles were made for suspension. The types of vessel range from very large storage jars to fine small vessels. Some bear decoration in the form of pairs of large, deeply ridged semicircles round the shoulder of the vessel known as 'eye-brow' decoration.

A site producing wares of considerable significance is the 'lake' village of Meare in the Somerset levels. These are late in the phase and their ceramic forms and decorations copy wooden or metal vessels. These vessels, both in form and decoration, show influences and origins drawn from a very wide area. One decorative form was derived from the classical palmette scroll, and it was used on vessels of similar periods at Cammaccio, Italy, and Mayer, Germany, at Stanlake, Middlesex, and at Balmadella, Scotland. It is also the commonest form of decoration on the metalwork of the period, and good examples can be seen on the various pieces from the Thames. The other basic form of decoration is the running 'S' scroll which occurs mainly on material from the 'lake' village at Glastonbury. In this instance a wide variety of abstract designs are grooved into the body of the vessels.

Intricate patterning is not limited to the south-west, for similar but restrained and more angular forms are seen on the shoulders of vessels from Southend-on-Sea, the West Midlands and Leicester.

Towards the end of the period the full flood of the effect of wheel-throwing is seen in the improvement of fabrics, thinner sections, and well-defined profiles, and from this emerged the three main types of vessel: a large, oval jar with pierced lug handles, which has been burnished all over except for a band across the middle which is decorated with cross-hatched burnished lines, a squat, drum-shaped bowl with a turned-out collar terminating in a bead rim, and a small, flat, round dish with straight raised sides.

The 'B' forms do not finish with the Roman invasions, nor is this the end of the Iron Age story, for interwoven with it is the coming of the 'C' or Belgic period.

IRON AGE 'C' (BELGIC)

Fabric Very fine, in some instances wholly untempered
Method of manufacture Usually thrown on the wheel and engine-turned while in the leather state
Firing Almost certainly fired in a specially constructed reducing kiln. White coarsewares do occur in this period but are considered to be imports
Principal characteristics Fine quality, well thrown and well turned vessel of predominatly black colour, with the whole tenor of manufacture and decoration being on the ability to turn

These people and their culture spread here from what is now Belgium, where they had achieved an advanced state of the La Tène culture and had also adopted and modified the growing influences of classical Rome, whose imports profoundly affected their art forms and ceramic techniques.

The Belgic settlements and invasions were initially concentrated in the south-east, especially in Kent, Essex and Hertfordshire, and towards the end of the first century BC they were spreading their area of activity. The primary examples of the culture are found in these areas, but the influences spread into the areas nearest to them.

Of major importance was the introduction of the wheel, which probably came in with this sub-culture and has already been discussed. The Belgae had considerable skill in turning, as can be seen on examples made of metal, wood and stone. This lathe-turning technique is reflected in the pottery forms, which were thrown to reproduce metallic or wooden forms. After being thrown on the wheelhead the vessel was allowed to dry to the leather state and was then put back on the head to which it was secured with a bed of clay; the excess clay was removed with a tool to give a sharp, clean surface, while at the

Page 87 (right) Romano-British 'Castor ware'. A colour coated beaker showing charioteers driving a quadriga. Unprovenenced. (below) Pagan Saxon Buckleurnen from Kempton with applied arcades, cruciform and ring and dot stamps within a grooved pattern.

Page 88 (right) Saxo/Norman Stamford ware. A spouted pitcher in white fabric with a pale orange glaze overall. From Oxford. (below left) Medieval Jug-of-London type influenced by North French wares, decorated with white and red slip and copper green wash under a lead glaze. From Bishopsgate, London. (below right) Post-medieval 'Metropolitan Ware'. A chamber pot made in or near Harlow, Essex. Decorated with white slip under a lead glaze.

same time horizontal grooves and beads were formed as decorative media. The vessels were also set upside down and the foot-rings were turned to a sharp profile.

The decoration of this period is relatively sparse with some cross-hatched and burnishing similar to that seen on the 'B' forms. Overall burnishing of a high order is commonplace. Some of the vessels are reduced to a grey rather than a black colour. The quality of this colouring is equal to that of the black colouring and is specially achieved. Another decorative form is 'rouletting', which is undertaken by the transference of a pattern cut on a small revolvable disk, by spinning it against the outside of the vessel. Such rouletting on vessels of this period is light in touch and simple in form, mainly copying grooving or cross-hatching.

The range of vessels produced is considerable, from large storage jars to globular cooking pots, and from small bowls to flat turned platters. This type of vessel was new to our history and was produced as the result of contacts with Rome, from which source came similar plates in the familiar 'black and red gloss wares' (known as *terra nigra* and *terra rubra*) which were imported in some quantities to this country. Such wares are stamped with the names or marks of the potter. Belgic potters copied these wares and imitated the stamps of the imports.

The Iron Age way of life abruptly changed with the Roman invasions. In the far north 'A' forms continued, with the 'B' forms universally established through the rest of England, and the outward influences of wheel turning had such a profound effect that even in those areas where the wheel was not yet in use, attempts were made to copy the forms that can only be produced by that method. In the south and south-east Rome began to show its ceramic influence, and there was a growing need for a wider variety of domestic vessels.

The Romano-British Period

Fabrics A wide variety of fabrics from coarse to wholly untempered. In each case, however, the fabric was deliberately

constructed to serve the purpose for which it was required
Method of manufacture Throwing on the wheel. Turning, spin
moulding, forming and modelling
Firing In single-flue and some parallel-flue kilns
Principal characteristics Wheel-thrown, mechanical forms, with
a wide variety of modest decoration, mostly of slip forms. In
the main the native wares are very plain except for the later
phases. A wide variety of ceramic forms of all kinds

The Roman invasion of AD 43 introduced the influence of an
industrialised society to this country. Since the development of
civilised communities in the Neolithic period, such civilisation
had grown and developed in the Mediterranean to reach a peak
of perfection in the Roman civil and military government; it
was at this pitch that ordered civilisation was spread by force
into the northern countries. Arriving on these shores as a
military machine, it came complete with all the efficiency
required to maintain a standing army requiring regular supplies
of familiar material, and amongst the standard issue were pots.
Potters (*figularii*) were part of a legion's establishment The first
phase of occupations are marked by military pottery and
quartermasters' purchase of local wares. Following the first
phase of Roman military occupation, the spread of pottery
manufacture into civil life was rapid and was backed up by
massive importations from Gaul and other parts of the Roman
Empire. The final phase was the setting up of civilian potting
centres to supply the new cities growing in the countryside.
These potters produced quantities of stereotyped forms of a
wide variety. Yet, despite this massive production, these wares
had little to offer to our ceramic history in general. Like much
else of the Roman occupation, its pottery came as a plant that
bloomed in profusion, but set no seed and died without issue. It
left no trace on our development, and when Rome departed,
so did the skills and techniques that it brought.

The main introduction was the use of kilns for firing wares
and the association of factory production at least in the legionary potteries. The kilns were single-flue updraught of all types
and sizes, sufficient for the needs of the occasional country
potter and those of the large industrial supplier. The other form

was the parallel-flue kiln, which was used for the production of roof tiles, building materials and heavy ceramics. Even though these kilns have a long history, they are relatively primitive, and their control needs to be thoroughly understood, knowledge gained probably by long practice, such as would be provided by an apprenticeship. Romano-British potters seem to have had this form of understanding of the control of their kilns, for in general their products are reasonably uniform in finish, no matter in what part of the country they were produced. This level of competence is relative when considering the poor quality of the products from similar kilns when they were reintroduced in the late Saxon period. It is possible that potting and other trades were set up as the result of special training of the natives by the conquerors.

In addition to the introduction of the kilns, we see a considerable improvement in manufacturing and decorative techniques. The preparation of the clays was in most cases very refined. The quality of many of the fabrics suggests that the process of washing (levigation) was used to separate the roughage from the clay and produce a perfectly smooth fabric of a given grain size free from any additives. In those vessels with strong native ties, sand tempering is commonplace, but in the other wares the quality of the fabric is good and often untempered. In many cases the standard of preparation is too high for the type of vessel produced. As the period progresses, we see a tendency to higher and higher firing temperatures, so that by the middle of the period some wares are already very hard, and at the end there are some groups of wares that are hard enough to produce a metallic ring when struck.

The manufacturing techniques were varied, for we find large ceramics of all kinds being coil-built. Slabbing was introduced for the production of oval-shaped flat dishes, splay-sided troughs, and other rectangular vessels. Wheel-throwing, however, was the dominant method of manufacture, and although post-thrown turned decoration is common, this was done in the wet state mostly and never again with the crisp assuredness of leather-state turning as practised by the Belgic potters. Casting by pouring slip into preformed moulds seems to have had a very limited use in the production of figurines. Both spin and press moulding are met with but are not common —the former for the production of standardised bowls and the latter for masks and small sprigged decoration and for the piece-moulding of foot-rings and other additional items, which were then luted on to the vessels required. Handles are sometimes pulled, but the commonest form is that rolled in a 'dolly box' mould from which the resultant decorated strip was lifted and applied.

The decoration of Romano-British vessels exhibits great variety and complexity and can occur as a single theme using only one method or in concert with other forms of decoration on the same vessel; it is quite common to see more than two or three types of decorative media being used on the same vessel together.

The use of slip has the widest form of application in this period. This can occur as a dipped partial or complete cover, as brush-applied or as trailed in a wide variety of coloured clays. In the earliest phase the use of white or cream slip is the commonest, especially on flagons. There are two forms of slip decoration which are unique to the Roman period. One is the application to the outside of a carefully prepared and sufficiently dried vessel of a thick piped body-colour slip to produce a bold and competent series of anthropomorphic and zoomorphic designs. The method by which this was achieved has been likened to that used in icing a cake, but it was based upon the condition of the vessel to be decorated and the viscosity of the slip rather than the method by which it was applied. I am assured that such results can be achieved by a variety of simple methods, with an emphasis on the skill required to fulfil them. The motifs are commonly simple scrolls, and less commonly complex hunting scenes of dogs, hare, and deer in magnificent assemblages which appear to flow about the pots on which they are laid. Known but quite rare are other more complicated figures, words or phrases.

The other slip decorative method unique to this period is

the use of slips with a high iron content to provide a distinct form of colour coating. These slips were prepared by the careful washing and segregation of parts of the slip to be used. Vessels dipped into these slips will give a wide range of colours, from jet black to bright orange, often with a high sheen, produced without any other aids such as burnishing or glazing.

The separation of clays with certain properties capable of producing this result had long been in use by Roman potters and others in northern Italy and at three places in Gaul. Known incorrectly as Samian ware, it was imported into this country in vast quantities. At Colchester there was a Samian (also known as *terra sigillata*) manufactory, set up by immigrant potters, which produced wares of inferior quality to those made on the Continent. Samian is in effect a glossy, colour-coated ware, the gloss being caused by the presence of illite in the clay. These wares are also red, as they are from an iron-derived source and were fired in a completely controlled oxidising atmosphere. In the early years of occupation, some red wares were produced known as *terra rubra*, and some known as *terra nigra*, which are black, being the reduced versions of the *terra rubra* forms. The black versions were so popular as to be widely imitated. Such black wares were also produced during the middle of the second century AD and are known as black Samian. The rapid establishment of the potting industry in the wake of the conquest soon made the general run of imports unnecessary, with the exception of Samian and the early types which continued up to about AD 60.

Another decorative motif restricted to this period is the use of mica to give a lustrous sheen to the outside of the vessels. These were dusted while still wet with mica crushed to a fine powder. The vessels were then burnished to a fine polish; in doing this the micaceous flakes were laid parallel to the surface and acted as a reflector. This practice is clearly an attempt to imitate metal forms and simulate the appearance of gold or bronze.

Burnishing was a very common practice throughout the whole 400 years of Roman occupation, and it carried on the

Iron Age 'B' tradition of the cooking pot, of burnishing all but a central band, which was then decorated with cross-hatching. There is evidence to show that burnishing was done on a wheel as well as by hand.

Applied pieces were commonly used in the form of pellets or strips and bands, or as representations of the deities and gladiators. Often these are very stylised. A special type of this group was a face vase, a vessel with a considerable ancestry and often associated with the burial of the dead. In some early forms the vessels are 'rusticated' by the application of very wet lumps of clay on to the surface which were then lifted by suction from the palm of the hand or with a bat to give an irregularly roughened surface. This was the typical cooking pot of some areas in the first century and it survived well into the second century.

The use of rouletting and stamping was very common throughout the whole period, especially at the end when stamping became more profuse on some types, such as flagons and bowls. These designs are limited to geometric forms such as circles and crosses.

Lead-glazing is known on vessels imported from St Remy in France during the first century and the technique was copied in Britain and is occasionally found on vessels produced as late as the end of the second century AD. The value of the quality and varieties possible with this medium seems never to have been appreciated, and the oxidised firing of a poor-quality lead glaze on a body rich in iron created an unfortunately muddy finish. The amount of lead-glazing is very limited, and does not appear ever to have been popular.

Potters' marks, common on the imported wares such as Samian and amphorae, are limited in this country to the makers of mortars (*mortarian*). In this case the potter had a stamp with his name or trade mark or some other means of identification, which he placed across the upper side of the rim of the vessel. Other potters' marks occur in the form of so-called batch marks, which usually take the shape of a roughly drawn parallel-armed cross which can also be set within a circle.

These are thought to be merely an indication of quantity, and they occur also in the Middle Ages in exactly similar form. However, such cross markings also occur in the late stages of the Iron Age and also throughout the Saxon period on vessels which one would consider were not made *en masse*. A common feature of the Roman period is the marking of vessels by the owner who frequently ascribed some mark or tally, presumably to define his own property. Amongst the military this was common and doubtless necessary. The makers of mortars stamped their wares with their names, which gives us a large number of Celtic personal names that have not been obtained from any other source.

A marked feature of this period is the range of body colours obtained by the use of controlled atmospheres. The whole range is met, with black through the red shades to the whitest white. Each potter fired his wares with a high degree of control, so that in every case he produced wares of a standardised finish. Black is common for cooking pots, shades of grey for other domestic wares and even for fine wares, and red is popular for domestic and very fine wares. White is used for mortaria, flagons and other domestic fine wares. Whatever colour is produced, it is usually clean and uniform on the vessel.

The black wares predominate, and many of these have distinctive sand tempering. Many are burnished and are known as 'black burnished' wares. These wares stem directly from the Iron Age 'B' and 'C' wares, common to the south of England at the time of the invasion. A steady development of these wares can be traced right up to the end of the occupation. The strength of the native tradition is marked by the refusal to abandon the traditional storage jars, cooking pots and platters, which remained although gradually changing in form.

The range of vessels during the period can be broken down as follows:

FLAGONS Up to 37cm high. Tall cylindrical neck with a reeded rim all above a globular body standing on a foot-ring. Handle fastened from rim straight down to the body.

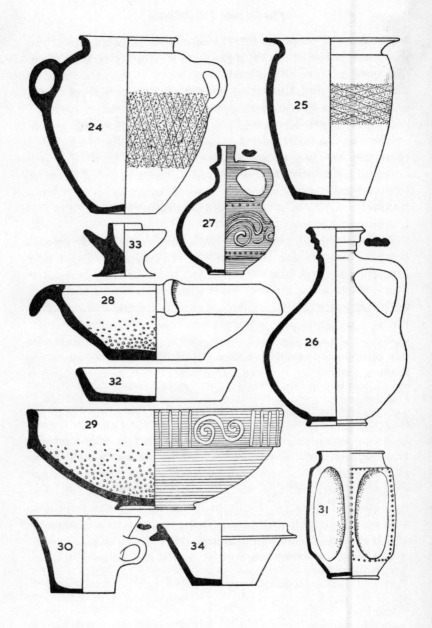

JARS   A wide variety of forms ranging from large, hand-built storage jars up to 1.5m high, to small domestic varieties of generally ovoid form about 22cm high.

BEAKERS   During the whole period of the occupation these are a constant feature, beginning with the Gallo-Belgic 'butt' beaker. The vessels at whatever part of the period follow the same pattern of being about 15–20cm high, with a narrow base and mouth and a globular middle. By the third century these shapes can vary a little and are often highly decorated.

TANKARDS   Another popular form from the second century was a drinking vessel, deriving from a Durotrigian form, shaped like a plant-pot with a ring-form handle, one or two fingers wide, to one side. Tankards are frequently decorated with burnishing and cross-hatching.

24–34   Romano-British types

24   Cooking pot, early second century AD. 'Black-burnished' with a central portion not burnished but with a lattice pattern incised on.

25   Cooking pot, late fourth century AD. 'Black-burnished' with an unburnished zone embellished with an incised lattice pattern.

26   Flagon, first century AD, in creamy coloured fabric. No decoration.

27   Flagon, late fourth century AD. In a white fabric, covered with a black slip over which has been trailed an abstract pattern in white slip.

28   Mortar, first century AD, with a pouring gully (only one side shown) and grit inside for grinding.

29   Mortar, late fourth century AD. No pouring gully or spout. Gritted interior. The outside coated with slip to give a red finish and the outside of the rim painted with a white slip pattern.

30   Tankard, second century AD, in a grey burnished fabric.

31   Beaker, third century AD, in a brown slipped fabric ('colour-coated ware') decorated with self-colour applied dots.

32   Dish, black burnished fabric. A standard form of vessel throughout the Occupation.

33   Candle-stick.

34   Flanged bowl, late fourth century AD. 'Black-burnished ware.'

COOKING POTS   These come in a wide variety of forms and sizes and comprise jars with the mouth narrower than the base and often with a lid seating. They are mainly, if not always, tempered in a fabric and fired black.

JUGS   Similar in shape to flagons, but with flaring vase-shaped necks and often copying the metallic forms.

MORTARIA   A type of vessel typical of this period, used for the grinding of soft foods to a paste. They come in the form of large heavy bowls with pronounced rims for lifting and also have spouts which appear to have been formed on a mould. On the inside of the base is set a layer of grits, usually of some sharp siliceous material, often using crushed quartz rock.

DISHES and PLATTERS   A wide variety of forms, the commonest being small and circular with vertical raised edges. Oval dishes with handles at both ends are also common. These vessels also spring from Gallo-Belgic traditions and are frequently made in tempered and wholly reduced fabrics.

COLANDERS (or WINE STRAINERS)   Specially made round-bottomed bowls with pronounced flange rims. Often with the piercings made in patterns.

CANDLESTICKS   Usually decorated with slip or in a fine turned fabric. They are of solid construction and sit on a built-in drip tray.

LAMPS   Although apparently mostly imported, there is some evidence for the manufacture of these piece-moulded forms in Britain. Hollow, heart-shaped vessels with a flat base, they have a handle at one end, a filling hole and a wick-hole. The upper surface is frequently decorated with a motif-bearing medallion.

LAMP FILLERS   Sometimes erroneously called 'baby feeders', these are small jars with narrow mouths, with a small teat to one side from which the oil can be poured.

LIDS   Many vessels are equipped with lid seatings, and thrown lids are common. They all take the same form of an inverted shallow flared dish on a small foot, which when turned over becomes the knob handle. Many similarly formed shallow bowls and dishes that occur during this period could thus have had a dual purpose.

INKWELLS Specially thrown to form a drum-shaped vessel with an internal flap as a trap to prevent spilling if the vessel is knocked over. Some also have holes set in the top to act as quill rests. Such vessels are a very rare form of Samian.

FUNERARY URNS It was common to bury a wide variety of domestic goods with the dead, a practice in which ceramics played an important part. However, most of the vessels were not specially manufactured for this purpose, with the exception of one type of jar with the representation of the human face upon it, which is found only in graves. These may be derived from the ancient custom of placing funerary masks or portraits of the deceased in the tomb.

These, then, are the principal domestic items produced. As with some other periods, it must be realised that this is only the general picture, for there are many themes and many variations on them, in the great mass of ceramics produced during the 400 years of Roman occupation of Britain.

A feature of this vast industrial achievement not yet discussed is the production of building materials. It is probably for this purpose alone that the parallel-flue kiln was used here. The major products appear to be roof tiles which were made to a standard form, comprising a flat, flanged and interlocking tile. These were laid upon the roof flat, raised edge to raised edge, each unflanged edge interlocking with the other, the flange being upstanding. These upstanding edges were then covered with slightly tapered half-round tiles, which fit into one another. This form of roof covering has a long history and its complexities reach a peak in the Grecian period, where there are many variations of the interlocking principles, brought down to a fine and simple conclusion by Roman austerity. Many of the Romano-British examples bear the stamps of the source of manufacture; in many cases these are military, for instance LEG. XX.VV. for the twentieth legion which was at Chester, and CL.BR. for the Romano-British Fleet, which seemed to spend its off-duty periods making tiles for the building trade. Other stamps were made by municipalities like London, or by private potters such as one at Letocetum (Wall, Staffs), who marked his tiles with the stamp PS. In military establishments the roofs were further embellished with antefixes, which are triangular plaques with a foot at the rear. These were inserted into the terminal tegulae at gutter level. The plaque fronts were often decorated with a stamped relief; in the case of the 20th Legion this was a rampant boar.

Other ranges of flat tile were normal for most civil sites, being used for bonding in building work, for floor coverings, and for piles for supporting the floors of hypocausts. Occasionally these tiles also bear the stamp of the makers. The use of the hypocaust system of heating requires the fumes and heat to be carried away and around the room to be heated. This was achieved through the use of 'flue tiles'. Such tiles are hollow rectangles with scoring on the outside to give a key or site for the wall plaster which was to cover them. In some places these tiles are finely decorated; in Leicester, for instance, they have fine stamped decoration in the form of woodland scenes with deer and other fauna.

Special though not uncommon forms of tile occur as voussoirs, sometimes with moulded reliefs. Less common are chimney-pots, or ornamental mouldings for string courses and other decorative constructional features.

Drain and sewage pipes were made with one end flanged to fit into the other. Such pipes were also used to carry water from pumping stations and were set into blocks of concrete for reinforcement. Such pipes were thrown, and as they are in the main long and narrow, a high degree of skill was required to produce them.

All of the techniques, types and forms discussed here occurred during the whole period of the occupation. It would seem that there was 'instant industry', at least within the first twenty-five years of the occupation, when the full force of it was being felt in southern Britain. By the beginning of the second century AD the foundation of cities and towns in addition to the great

military establishments stimulated the growth of local in-
dustries; both large and small are found widely distributed.
There is considerable evidence to show that potteries operating
in the North and East Midlands were supplying the quartermasters' orders for the Wall forts. In this century also there
was a vast pottery industry at Petersfield, Hampshire, supplying
the needs of Winchester and Chichester. By the third century
major centres were beginning to form in the Nene valley, at
Doncaster, Lincoln, Oxford and in the New Forest, the first
and the last of these being the largest factory areas. Colchester,
too, had a large potting centre, with a variety of kilns, some of
which appear to be double-flued. The Nene valley, Oxfordshire, and the New Forest have a quality and variety un-
surpassed by the products of other kilns. The vessels are well
made and finely decorated wares, which had a currency over a
considerable area. Thus by the fourth century there were well-
established major potting centres mostly near towns, but also
widespread through the country though usually not far from
the main communities. The use of both factory- and country-
made pottery was commonplace; no home was without a wide
variety of ceramic vessels upon which much depended in the
preparation and serving of food. In fact throughout the whole
of the Roman occupation we see a society dependent upon the
production of pottery as a supplement to its daily needs, and
yet by the end of the fourth century AD the collapse of the
Roman Empire was to shatter this system of dependence.

The pressures of the Saxons upon the northern frontiers of
the Empire brought the Romans to rely upon a wide variety of
military assistance, and amongst those brought to England were
many Germans, whose ceramic requirements were similar to
those found throughout north-western Germany. These vessels
were of special form and decoration and they created a new
demand for the local potter wherever their users were stationed
or settled in groups. There arose as a result a group of wares
known as Romano-Saxon wares which are wheel-thrown and
kiln-fired, and which copy the Saxon forms and decorations.
Such wares occur during the fourth century and are found

mainly in the area around East Anglia. Examples are few, and they are not followed by any other developed form; they illumine the end of an epoch.

The end of Roman rule can be equated not only with the end of central government, but also with the end of markets and the structure of civilisation that was orientated to the use of materials that it could no longer obtain. In some areas this lack of purpose-made pottery led to attempts to produce hand-made wares, and these are being increasingly recognised, especially in the west of England, as being commonplace to the period around and after AD 360. The change from Roman to Saxon occupation is complex and as yet not fully understood. What is apparent is that the use of Romano-British factory-made pottery ceased abruptly sometime during the first half of the fifth century over a wide area of England, and while hand-made pottery is known to have been made at this time, enough is not yet known about it to say what it was like. The total destruction of this simple craft must have been brought about entirely because the Saxon settlers' way of life was vastly different from that of the Romano-British. The Saxons did not require anything other than those things that they understood, and machine-made, kiln-fired pottery was not among these. As a result the knowledge of mechanised potmaking died, amongst a host of other civilising things.

The Dark Ages, the Celtic West and the Pagan Saxons

The Saxon occupation of the British Isles was never completed, if that had ever been their intention. That which finally became Saxon by the end of the sixth century had taken some 150 years to complete and consolidate. Wales west of the Severn, the western peninsula, firstly west of Mendip and then west of Dartmoor, all of Cumberland and Strathclyde, the more remote northlands, all of Scotland, Ireland and the Isle of Man, are the vast parts of these islands that were never occupied. This region is now known as the Celtic West, and has only recently come under the scrutiny and interest of the archaeologist, the result of whose work shows two points of interest. One is that pottery was certainly made for some time after the break with Rome, but mainly of the crude hand-made forms that we saw in the late Roman period. It seems as if a break occurred in the local potting traditions of sufficient length for the tradition of the wheel and the kiln to have been lost, even though in certain places such manufacturing did continue in the old tradition up to the sixth century. Information on this important part of our history remains slight, and we are still in a period of prognostication from which at the moment little reliable fact can be sifted from a good deal of supposition. The other point of interest is that despite the relative fastness of the Celtic West and the fact that by the end of the sixth century local production had virtually ceased, these people were still pottery-users. Although less dependent on ceramics, they used wares imported from the Mediterranean and the western French littoral. It is thought that some of these wares bore a strong religious significance, having reproductions of crosses, fishes and hares upon them, for these people had remained Christian from their conversion under Constantine. Many of the pottery fragments are of amphorae, but there are also bowls, flasks, platters and similar vessels in fine-quality red or cream coloured unglazed earthenwares which would suggest domestic as well as religious usage. The amount of this material is relatively small and this might suggest that after the end of the fifth century the use of domestic ceramics was restricted to those who could afford what had by this time become a luxury.

This does not in any way answer the great mystery of why pottery manufacture, either by the wheel and kiln or by reversion to a completely hand-made type, ceased altogether in areas that were lived in by people accustomed to using pottery wares for all the preceding centuries since the Neolithic. This unlearning was so profound that in many parts of the Celtic West it was not restored until the Middle Ages.

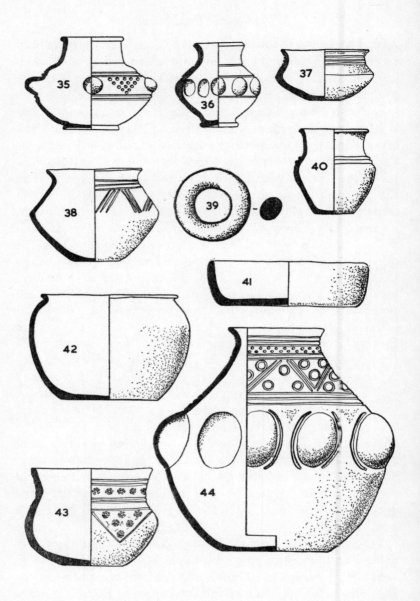

THE PAGAN SAXONS

Fabric In the early stages fine, sand- and grass-tempered, showing a decline in quality towards the end of the period

Method of manufacture Hand-made, probably solely by the lump method

Firing In the early stages certainly fired in controlled clamp kilns of equal quality to those of the Iron Age 'B' period, declining as does the fabric due to less controlled circumstances

Principal characteristics Ranging from fine to poorer during the whole phase commencing with very fine well-made wares with groove, slashing, embossing and stamping decoration

The pagan Saxons had settled in most of England other than the Celtic West by the sixth century. They originated along the north-western German littoral from Jutland to the Frisian Islands. These people lived in a late Iron Age 'B' tradition and ceramically they fit well into that milieu. Their pottery was hand-built and fired in a controlled reducing clamp. The wares are well-made and some are well-burnished, both without and within the vessel, so that their arrival and domination of the ceramic field carries us back one step in time. Such is the similarity with the Iron Age wares that for years many of the early wares of this period were thought to be of that period.

The wares fall into two distinct types, domestic and funerary.

35–44   Romano-Saxon and Pagan-Saxon types

35, 36   Romano-Saxon types, late fourth and five centuries AD. Wheel-thrown with bosses and indented decoration in the Pagan Saxon manner.

37–42   Pagan Saxon types hand-made wares, some with burnishing on the upper parts. Decorated with grooving (37 and 38) or with ridges (40). These are the commonplace vessels that exist from the turn of the fourth century AD. Into the seventh century AD.

43, 44   Two types of vessel showing the use of decorative techniques, of which 43 is common domestic type and 44 is a ritual funerary piece known as *Buckelurnen*. Both these wares are hand-made, burnished on the upper part or completely. The decoration takes the form of stamps, grooves or pushed-out bosses.

The domestic wares, although they can be very fine, are in general crude in finish and declined rapidly soon after the settlement was established. Many of the wares are burnished, although in the larger examples burnishing occurs only on the upper surfaces of the vessel, and in many cases the lower portions were left quite rough, another indication of the possibility of lump manufacture. Some vessels were tempered with fine sandy material while others were tempered with grasses, a practice which increased in some areas and continued throughout the whole Saxon period. On domestic forms decoration is sparse and uncommon, but when used it takes a wide variety of forms, such as jabbing the finger into the wet clay quite roughly, or pressing out large, smooth, disk-shaped indentations, or finger or tooled grooving, or applying pieces in the form of small conical bossed and small grooved patterns. Special tooled effects include rouletting of small rectangular patterns and stamping of small but varied patterns of geometrical form, e.g. by stamping with a piece of wood over which a piece of cloth was placed to give the pattern of the weave.

There is variation not only in the decorations but also in the pottery forms, which have been classified as follows: pedestal-footed bowls; biconical bowls (these have the sharp-angled profile which is an early feature of this period); globular jars without rims; globular jars with collared rims (these are the commonest forms); and wide-mouthed globular jars. Drinking vessels occur as semi-globular and biconical beakers. There are also flat-walled circular dishes, colanders and lids. All these wares have flat bases, and although not all early wares are flat-based the majority appear to be so; the tendency to rounder bases increased as the period progressed.

Also in the domestic field are spindle whorls and loom-weights, the former being small disks each 10cm in radius with a centrally pierced hole into which the spindle was fastened. The loom-weights of this period are 'doughnut' shaped and about 22cm across; like the spindle whorls they were hand-made and very roughly fired. There is sufficient evidence to show that these were used to work on an upright loom of similar pattern to that used during the Iron Age 'A' period. Occasionally unbaked examples of such loom-weights have been found, suggesting that not all were fired before use.

Funerary vessels known as *Buckelurnen*, although occurring at the same period, are strikingly different to the domestic wares. They are about 30cm high, large enough to take the bones of a cremated mature adult. They can be round and globular in shape, or biconical with flat bases and sometimes with foot-rings. They are usually very well made by hand in a fine, sandy-tempered fabric; during building they had large bosses and lozenge-shaped bulges raised round the outsides at irregular intervals. The raising of horizontal ridges is also common. These vessels are often highly burnished and they were fired completely reduced, to produce a black and shiny effect. The burnishing and embossing is further embellished with grooving of the surface, which takes the form of pendent triangles. Such joint forms are considered to be the earliest decorative media. By the sixth century stamp decoration was added and bosses declined, the grooving became more precise, stamp decoration increased and the variety of stamped forms widened until, by the seventh century, stamping was the main form of decoration. With the coming of Christianity at this time the manufacture of funerary urns ceased altogether.

About the end of the seventh century we enter the Middle Saxon period, of which as yet little can be said for England as a whole, for there is nothing substantial upon which to fix a pointer to the general forms and features of the types. It is known, however, that pottery was generally in decline throughout this period; the fabric and the number of types were both reduced to the utmost simplicity. Globular cooking pots and beakers are known to have continued, but other forms disappeared. In some regions grass tempering became the popular medium. The basic form of the vessels changed from flat to globular, and in some areas vessels were wholly globular with no definition of a base as such. Much of this type of ware continued to be made in England with certain special exceptions up to the tenth century, and in some of the remoter areas even later, only to be changed with the introduction of medieval wares.

However, in East Anglia following the coming of Christianity a remarkable sequence of events took place that was to alter the ceramic sequence entirely. At this time East Anglia was the most highly populated area in England with several important and thriving towns. The town of Ipswich was a port which traded with the Rhineland. From this source new types of pottery, some with 'classical' profiles, were introduced and with them returned the single-flue updraught kiln. Since Roman times the potters' craft had continued to flourish unchanged along the banks of the lower Rhine—as it has continued to do to this day—and the trade with that area, at first importing pots, was bound in time to import potters: and so it proved at Ipswich. The first pottery to be introduced was of Frisian type and consisted of small cooking pots; also larger but similarly shaped vessels but with strap handles and small spouts set just under the rim called 'pitchers'; also small open bowls. This pottery does not appear to have been thrown on a conventional wheel but to have been made on a turntable of some simple kind that gave it a somewhat ungainly form. These wares were fired in a kiln that gave some reduction, and they are mainly grey in colour. Their distribution appears to be limited to East Anglia, and they remained the sole types in use for over two hundred years.

The Late Saxon and Norman Periods

Fabrics Two distinct forms current at different places and sometimes at the same place. One coarse sand or grass tempering, the other very fine, possibly wholly untempered
Method of manufacture Hand and wheel
Firing In kilns and in controlled clamps, giving a wide variety of results, depending upon the materials handled
Principal characteristics Coarsewares of globular form, mostly cooking pots. Very fine wares both glazed and unglazed in a wide variety of forms. The growth of wheel-thrown if not of kiln-fired materials

Towards the middle of the ninth century another wave of Rhenish influences was felt in East Anglia. Major potting centres had been set up at Badorf to supply the needs of the growing export trade. Here the wheel was used, and its use returned to England about this time. It was first taken up at Ipswich, where the old traditional types continued to be made, but in refined forms. At the same time new forms were brought in, such as the large storage jar of up to 75cm in height, lamps which in this instance are small shallow bowls on stems similar to large egg-cups, and the costrel, a water bottle used by travellers—a common Romano-British ceramic type, it returned with its shape unchanged. What is quite remarkable is that the wheel and pottery improvements spread rapidly through that part of England known as the Danelaw, for in their homeland at this period the Danes used little or no pottery. It is of striking interest that many of the new forms that developed as a result of the introduction have latent classical shapes so reminiscent of Roman pottery; for many years much of this pottery was considered to be of that date. The potting centres grew up in East Anglia, each producing its own characteristic wares. Thetford ware is sandy and grey in colour; the forms are narrow-mouthed cooking pots, bowls and spouted pitchers. St Neots ware has a fabric type which was used in the East Midlands from Iron Age times, having a very high proportion of crushed shell as a tempering medium. Kilns have never been found for the production of this type, which consists of small pots and bowls with inturned rims. The ware is soft and purple in colour and was probably fired in controlled oxidising clamps. Kiln sites and pottery forms for this period have been found at Leicester, Torksey (Lincolnshire), and York. At Chester there is a very distinctive ware which was being made when the defences were being repaired at the beginning of the tenth century, and similar wares have been found at Tamworth, Shrewsbury and Hereford. Recently hard wheel-thrown wares have also been found in South Hampshire, so it would appear that a general outward movement of potting techniques was under way.

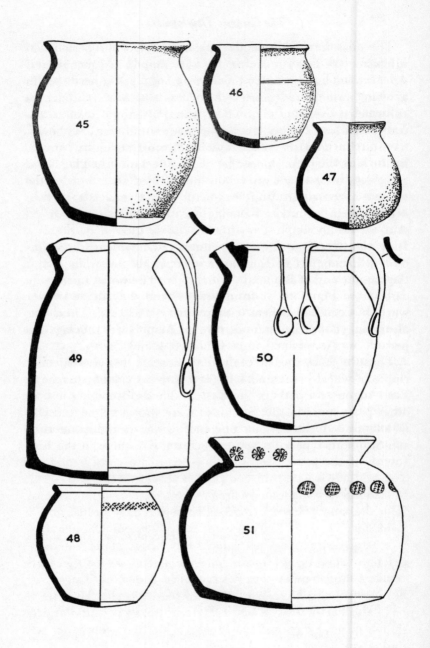

The most important centre in the history of the period and the history of English ceramics was Stamford in Lincolnshire. At this town a remarkably fine series of wares was produced in a white untempered fabric, glazed with lead and fired in a constructed oxidising kiln. These wares, although made in the traditional forms of cooking pots, spouted pitchers and bowls, have in the majority of cases a quality of the highest order, in the throwing, finishing and glazing techniques. Plain lead glaze was used to give a yellow finish, lead with iron mixed to give a red finish, and lead with copper mixed to give a bright green finish. Lead-glazing was not a suddenly acquired skill, for we know that it was being widely used in Byzantium, Italy and Greece at this time, countries with which Britain was by now in contact. The first town to copy this development was the capital city of England, Winchester. The potters probably came from Stamford or from France, and they made similar wares but decorated them with greater exuberance. There was also some floor tile manufacture at Winchester during this period, but from what source is not yet known.

Thus we see by the end of the tenth century an ever-widening ripple of wheel-made and kiln-fired wares, by then current in East Anglia and parts of the East Midlands, occurring also in other parts sporadically. Stamford ware was in vogue and was widely traded throughout England, while at the same time sub-Stamford-type kilns were appearing elsewhere in the East

---

45–51 Middle Saxon and Saxo-Norman types

45–7 Crude, hand-made wares fired in a reducing atmosphere. Eighth to tenth century.

48 Wheel-thrown ware decorated with rouletting. In a hard, grey, sandy fabric. Tenth century.

49 Jug. Wheel-thrown in a dark grey, hard sandy fabric with a wide pulled strap handle. Tenth or eleventh century.

50 Spouted pitcher with three handles. Stamford type. White fabric with a clear yellow lead glaze. Strap handle fixed with two deep thumb impressions. Eleventh or twelfth century.

51 Cooking pot in a buff sandy fabric decorated with stamps. West Sussex. Eleventh or twelfth century.

Midlands. But despite this seeming growth, it would appear to have been limited to the centres of population and the new and growing towns. There were, throughout the late Saxon period, areas where pottery was not used at all, as in some midland and northern areas, where it is common to find aceramic levels before the advanced stage of the Middle Ages.

The Middle Ages

Fabrics Starting generally mixed in quality from fine to poor, settling down to fine tempering mostly based on sandy fills by the end of the twelfth century
Method of manufacture Wheel and hand building. Slabbing and forming of heavy ceramics
Firing Double-flue updraught, multi-flue updraught, and parallel-flue kilns
Principal characteristics Reduction to two main types of domestic vessel—the jug and the cooking pot. Reintroduction of heavy ceramics. Introduction of building brick

During the eleventh century changes in pottery forms come into evidence. The cooking pot which in late Saxon times was mainly a narrow mouthed vessel, changed very rapidly to become a squat, wide-mouthed form; this new form spread widely through the rest of the century to become universal by the twelfth century and continued so through the rest of the period up to the fifteenth century. In East Anglia the pitcher, which was firmly established, increased in size and was translated to Winchester whence it spread to become the dominant water-carrying vessel in an area from Hampshire northwards to Worcestershire. Some of these pitchers acquired short stubby feet and are known as 'tripod pitchers'.

A more significant change was taking place at Stamford where a cylindrical jug with a single pulled strap handle and pulled spout began to be produced at the end of the eleventh century. These were the forerunners of the famous medieval jug that was to become the universal water-carrier in Britain for the next 250 years. It seems to have spread to the European mainland from this country, for there is no evidence there of such a similar development. Its antecedents are not plain. It could have been a direct and natural development at Stamford, but such things are always unlikely, and there were at this time vessels of similar form in common use in Italy, Greece and other places in the Mediterranean.

The Norman Conquest is marked in our ceramic history by a general and rapid, though short-lived, decline in quality. In some areas where there was definite improvement taking place, we see a sudden decline to poor-quality hand-made wares. Winchester and the area adjacent to it has striking evidence of this, where refined coarse wares were succeeded by poor-quality grass-tempered and grass-wiped wares. However, this change did no more than slow the developments of the period, for the late eleventh century and the twelfth saw the development of the wide-mouthed cooking pot, the spread of the tripod pitcher over wide areas, and the advent of the glazed jug spreading from Stamford. The decorations of this phase included scoring and combing of the surfaces, and wiping down the outside of the vessels with grass. Applied strips of various types were widely used, especially on the large storage jars of the south and East Anglia. Stamped decoration appears to have been commonly used in some restricted areas. Open lamps and crucibles occurred, and for the first time we see the manufacture of fire covers, a requisite by law for covering the fire during the curfew (*couvre feu*). By the end of the twelfth century the Stamford jug had become a glorious spectacle of splendid colour and applied decoration.

THE THIRTEENTH CENTURY

The thirteenth century is one of the highwater marks in our ceramic history. A great deal happened, particularly towards the end of the century, that was to have a profound effect on much that followed. It was in this century that widespread advances took place in art, architecture and industry. In ceramics we see firstly the development of two forms of kiln, the double-flue updraught and the multi-flue updraught, and the reintroduction of the parallel-flue kiln. The double-flue kiln spread from some source of specific development as yet unknown, to become widespread throughout southern England and sparsely spread in places north of the Trent. There are cases of three- and four-flued kilns known, and recent work on a major pottery-producing centre at Nuneaton has shown that it had all types. At this time, however, we are unable to show how the larger multi-flue updraught kilns developed or why they had such a strong influence on the potting of the north-east Midlands and south Yorkshire. In Yorkshire there was also at this time an individualistic type of kiln that produced very coarse wares; it consisted only of the pit into which the pot was placed with peat which was then fired.

The development of kilns went hand in hand with the growth of industry, and coal was often used in the period wherever it was readily available, as was peat.

The return of the parallel-flue kiln heralded the rapid production of heavy ceramics, a task for which it is admirably suited, but potters, being ingenious men, soon found that pots can be fired in these kilns, and that building materials can be fired in both double and multi-flue kilns. The parallel-flue kiln returned unchanged from its established classical form, arriving perhaps towards the end of the thirteenth century. It probably came from France or the Low Countries, where we know it was used in the thirteenth century, and again it is thought to have come in through East Anglia. The principal product of such kilns was roof furniture, flat, hip and ridge tiles. Louvers and chimney pots were also made. Floor tiles, both decorated and plain, became the trade of 'tyghlers', who travelled about making pavements for churches and great houses. Brick-making was also established at this time; the bricks were fired mainly in clamps in which the 'green' brick was packed in great specially constructed stacks interlaced with fuel which was ignited; the whole clamp burned off, leaving the bricks burned to an oxidising red colour.

Of the roof furniture mentioned above, two items are worthy of special note, the louvers and finials. Louvers sit on the crest of the roof and allow the fumes of the fire and house to pass out. They are nearly always constructed in the most individual fashion, and in some instances are highly decorated with glaze colours and applied decorative motifs of many kinds. However, they are outshone by the variety of decoration and form seen in the finials which decorated the gable-heads of even simple buildings. Many of these have human form and the faces are set in the most humorous of styles. Roof ridge tiles were also decorated with cut ridges which are shaped like coxcombs, crenelations, or in the form of hooks, according to the regions where the features are common. Regional variation was considerable throughout the whole of this period of the flowering of medieval potting.

By the thirteenth century the use of domestic ceramics had become universal once more. The quantity of production was enormous and the quality very variable. The principal types of vessel produced were the jug and cooking pot, but a range of other vessels were also produced, such as tripod pitchers, aquamanile (see below), pipkins, money boxes, spindle whorls, bowls, pans, skillets, dripping pans, mortars and other minor items.

Of these the most striking product was the medieval jug, which ranges in date through to the fifteenth century. Many of these products are highly decorated, some with every known technique on any earthenwares, with the exception of the colour blue and the use of tin in the glaze. Many are decorated in high relief with animal and human figures or just with representations of the human face. Stamped decoration is frequent and is of the widest form and complexity, as are the patterns obtained from elaborately carved roulette wheels. Incision and grooving are very common and in a few instances are used through a coloured slip to give a two-colour pattern. The use of coloured slips in a general, random or specific set of patterns was frequent, and so on through the whole gamut of possibilities. The form of the jugs varies from short and fat to tall and thin, and the handles and spouts also vary. Many are sagging-based, a deliberate feature and one common to both jugs and cooking

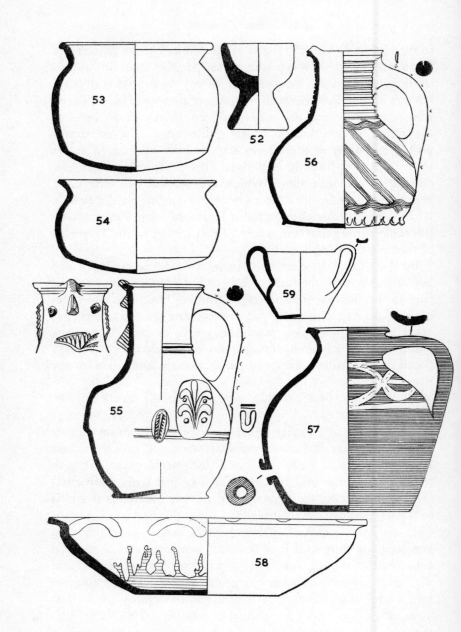

pots in this period—a traditional principle and one not easy to understand, as the bases have to be deliberately depressed to compensate for the instability thus caused to the jug. Many are provided with a separately applied foot-ring which is often crimped into a frilly edge.

Cooking pots, on the other hand, are much meaner in quality, even when they come from the same source that makes fine jugs. They appear to be the bread-and-butter line which changed but little and then only gradually throughout the whole of the Middle Ages.

Another form peculiar to the Middle Ages is a vessel known as an aquamanile, literally 'water for the hands'. These are often made in animal forms, standing square on their four feet with the tails coming back to make a handle. The hollow body is specially constructed with an internal trap to regulate the direction of the flow of water which issues from a tube in the

---

52–59 Medieval to late medieval types

52 Lamp in a hard, sandy, dark grey fabric. Of late Saxon type continuing well into the medieval period.

53 Cooking pot. Sandy red fabric. Throughout the thirteenth century.

54 Cooking pot. Hard sandy buff fabric, internal green glaze on the base only. Late fourteenth into the fifteenth century.

55 Jug (Rye, Sussex). Oxidised pink fabric, copper green glaze, stamped bosses. 'Face on front', decoration. Mid- to late thirteenth century.

56 Jug (West Sussex ware). Decorated with grooves on the neck and combing on the body under an iron green glaze. Fourteenth into the fifteenth century.

57 Cistern (painted ware). In a hard, untempered fabric. Unglazed. Decorated with white slip round the shoulders. Fired-reduced to give a black and white finish. Sussex, late fifteenth century.

58 Dish in an oxidised untempered fabric. Glazed inside on the base only. Decorated with white painted swags round the rim. Sussex. Late fifteenth century.

59 Cup, 'Tudor green'. Fine white fabric covered with a fine, high-quality copper green glaze. Surrey. Late fifteenth and sixteenth century.

mouth. Decoration runs riot on every kind of vessel in this period; it seems to occur mainly in the second half of the thirteenth century and through to the early part of the fourteenth.

Decline or rather simplification begins to be seen after this time. Ebullience was suppressed and decoration was reduced to geometric forms and other lighter styles. By the beginning of the fifteenth century decoration became sparse and in some areas vanished altogether. At this time we see the beginning of a break-up of established traditions. The whole of the fifteenth century sees the ceramic profession in turmoil. The most important outcome of a period of searching for new types was the final acceptance that it was possible to make pottery without the aid of tempering agents. This major factor and the break-up of medieval forms marks the start of a new period.

The Post-medieval period

Fabric Principally wholly untempered
Method of manufacture Wheel-made. Spin and press moulding. Casting. Forming, at the end of the period. Increasing use of mechanical aids
Firing Single-flue updraught kilns but an increase in the development of the bottle kiln, with the introduction of the downdraught kiln at the end of the period. Introduction of the sagger
Principal characteristics A phase of great change and rapid development with a notable improvement in quality of all types of ware, the majority of which are oxidised. Later in the period a distinct division of qualities. The introduction of English-made delfts and salt-glazes. The development of 'fine earthenwares'. The over-riding influence of Chinese porcelain

Towards the end of the fifteenth century the variety of ceramic products was legion, although becoming rapidly regionalised. In the north the wares remained basically medieval in form but of much more simplified type. From south Yorkshire down to the Midlands, although medieval forms also persisted, there was a period when they were sparsely glazed and fired very hard in a reducing kiln to give a dark purple colour to the vessel. These vessels are very crude in finish. A different development took place along the coast from East Anglia to Cornwall. The products were large pitchers with strap handles and a bunghole near the base; associated with these were deep dishes. These types were sometimes fired with a reduced finish, and many are decorated with a regionalised, white, brush-applied slip decoration. In Surrey the production of fine wares in a white fabric decorated with copper green or lead yellow glazes was developed, the products probably influenced by wares imported from Holland and France. These kilns produced for the London market, although their products were widely distributed.

The last quarter of the fifteenth century saw an important event, the massive importation of Flemish grey salt-glazed stoneware drinking mugs, of the type illustrated by Brueghel in 'The Wedding Feast'. Also in the early part of this century vessels made in a fine white fabric glazed to a bright green colour were imported from France. These took the form of cups, some of which are segmented shallow forms with one or more loop handles. These are the types so readily copied in Surrey and later at other potteries throughout England.

These ceramic developments all reflect a changed pattern of domestic usage; this is illustrated by the removal of the fireplace from the middle to the side or the end of the house, and the preparation of food on the hearth or in a pot hung from the chimney-piece. The change in cooking habits also coincided with a widening of the food horizon through increased foreign trade, further embellished and encouraged by a wider communication at certain levels of society with the habits of continental Europeans in general. The standards achieved in the great houses passed down the line to arrive modified, but still influential, at the peasant's hovel.

The strength of these changes is reflected most in the abandonment of the ceramic cooking pot, which had been an integral part of the domestic scene in an unbroken line back to the

Neolithic. This was replaced in the fifteenth and sixteenth centuries with a cast-iron pot, which copied the ceramic forms, and a shape was soon established in the iron forms which fossilised, so that vessels of this precise form continue to be made in the Black Country today. At the time of the change to metal vessels, some cooking pots were made by potters that copied the only special feature that the metal forms possess—an angular handle. This development was short-lived.

It is the area in which the multi-flue updraught kilns occur that is of next importance. Somewhere in Yorkshire in the second half of the fifteenth century there appeared, apparently quite suddenly, a developed group of wares consisting of cups, tankards and a wide variety of other vessels in a red fabric, glazed with lead which had been heavily filled with iron. This thickened glaze gives the vessels a range of rich black to brown hues. The vessels are frequently decorated with applied pieces of thick white slip, some of which are presented as animals and others applied as disks which were then stamped. The quality of these wares is very high, and so far no source of development has been discovered for them. Although they are closely linked to 'Midland purple' techniques, it is considered that they did not derive from this source, and it is possible that, like so much else, they came out of the Low Countries, where vessels of similar if not exactly parallel form and fine quality are known. The wares were fired in saggers, the first time such vessels had been used in England. As these wares were first recognised from the upper levels of occupation in the vast monastic establishments of Yorkshire, they were thought to have been made by the monks and so are called 'Cistercian wares'. It is now known that the monks did not generally pot in this or any other period in our history.

Throughout the sixteenth century, the great diversification of pottery forms merged throughout England to become more or less regularised, with distinct regional variations in colour and sometimes in shape, but the types of vessels and their use remained fairly constant. We see cups, tankards, dishes, skillets, storage jars, bowls, pancheons, ornaments and the whole range of heavy ceramics which are commonplace right up to the beginning of the twentieth century. Another form not common, but which began in this period, was the alembic, a form of still which consists of two pots, the lower one being a plain pan form with steep sides similar to a saucepan, with a pronounced lid seating, the upper one being conical, at the lower end of which was an internal flange; a spout on the outside of this lid was pierced through to the flange. When the contents of the pan were warmed, the steam rising would condense on the inside of the cone and run down the inside of the lid, into the flange, and through the spout. Such vessels probably made a crude form of spirit; 'brandywine' (burned wine) was coming into popularity at this period.

The end of the sixteenth century saw the beginning of the end of the long period of earthenware domination, for two changes took place which had considerable effect on the future. The first was the introduction of the Chinese porcelain trade, sparked off by the Portuguese trade from Macau. The second challenge to the earthenware tradition was the introduction of another potter's type known as maiolica or delft, a tin-glazed earthenware. At this point the history must split into three parts, for we have the continuance of earthenware, the introduction, flowering and decline of delft, and the introduction and brief flowering of stonewares, which in their way led to better things.

EARTHENWARES FROM THE END OF THE SIXTEENTH CENTURY

The earthenwares of the late sixteenth century are in general of very fine quality, and of a wide variety of forms. Most of them are well glazed and some are decorated with slip, although the majority with a few special exceptions are plain wares, except in the North and the West Midlands. The growth and popularity of the Cistercian forms developed, and they were being made as far afield as Herefordshire, Bedfordshire, Hampshire, Wiltshire and Essex by the middle of the sixteenth century.

The dish which we first saw as an introduction to the coast of eastern and southern England in the late fifteenth century had become a platter by the end of the sixteenth century and a plate by the middle of the seventeenth, by which time it was in universal use. At some time in the early seventeenth century these platters began to bear a wide variety of slip decorations. These, like other things, arrived as established forms, and again the source is not yet known. However, slip decoration of the type met with on these dishes was already highly developed on the Continent, and two sources from which influence must have come are the area around Frisia, where trailed slip patterns of a form familiar in Essex and Northamptonshire commonly occurred in the late sixteenth century, and Beauvais in northern France, where the decorative motif was to use 'sgraffito' to lay colour different from the body clay in slip form on the surface of the vessels, so that when cut down it revealed the contrasting body colour underneath. Such sgraffito is common to the western peninsula, where it has a long and honourable history. Here, not only was slip allowed to dry before being cut through, but at Bristol it was worked while wet, with the fingers, to give a similar but less harsh effect. Trailed slip, on the other hand, appears to have been confined to Essex, Northamptonshire, South Yorkshire and the North Staffordshire towns. Although the patterns differ from place to place, similar motifs can be seen in all of them, so there must be a link.

In the sixteenth century we see the growth of Burslem, a town sitting astride upturned seams of coal and vari-coloured clays, geographically well placed to serve the growing towns of the industrialising Midlands, South Lancashire and South Yorkshire, and with entry to the sea through the river Trent— a series of circumstances that placed it favourably for the coming boom.

By the middle of the seventeenth century slipwares were commonplace, in some areas—London, the Yorkshire–East Midland complex, North Staffordshire—and on some Surrey forms the decoration reached a high degree of competence and ebullience.

It was about the middle of the century that pottery-making centres began to arise, as opposed to the single potter making for one market. We begin to see not only centralised production, but for the first time some construction within the industry. Where fuel, clay, and people could be found or put together, there grew the trade, so we see the growth of potteries in London, Fareham, Plymouth, Bristol, Swansea, Buckley, Poole, Liverpool, Newcastle, Sunderland, the South Yorkshire coalfields and above all at Burslem, for by the end of the seventeenth century this small potting town had grown to such proportions that its wares were to have a tremendous effect over the whole of England. This was due mainly to the outward-looking attitude of the potters, who did something no other potting community in England had ever done before: put export before home consumption. It was the business acumen of the potters of Burslem that really made them famous, for in the early days of their potting history their wares were no better than any one else's, and they improved only with the growth of trade and competition. This condition did of course increase, sponsored the famous potters of the eighteenth century, and founded a trade whose products are sold around the world in greater quantity than in England.

During the latter half of the seventeenth century, there was a great movement spurred firstly by foreign influences and secondly by casting off the Commonwealth yoke, that led to the production of a wide variety of fine-quality domestic materials, which included ceramics, and from about 1670 we see serious attempts to improve earthenwares, a move which was also stimulated by the growing threat of delfts and maiolic. At this time the Restoration gave rise to a welter of patriotic feeling, which in turn led to the production of cabinet pieces of highly decorative nature, picturing kings and queens and regal symbols, as well as facsimiles of Adam and Eve. Such vessels were produced mainly by the Toft school, and, remarkable as they are as pieces of considerable skill in trailed decoration, they add little to our knowledge of the products of the multitude of other slipware potters, whose wares lie un-

honoured and unsung, but none the less remain a true reflection of the public taste of the period. Cabinet pieces were also made in delft, using similar motifs, and it is possible that the Toft plates and the steady improvements in the other slipware products show that the pressure of competition was being felt. Although delft was made in several places in England it was never made at Burslem.

What this competition eventually did was to sort the wheat from the chaff. Second-rate fine wares could not be foisted off on a public with a wider choice, and poor potters were relegated to making coarse wares, while the rest and especially those in Burslem, London and South Yorkshire worked to improve their wares. This they did to good effect, as the products of the first half of the eighteenth century show. These wares are of a fine quality, with modest and restrained decorative motifs in slip, in brown, black or mottled finishes. The glazes are improved and clarified, and controlled with the

---

60–68 Post-medieval types

60 'Cistercian ware'. Hard, dark red fabric. Glaze stained dark with iron. Decorated with applied pads of white slip. Yorkshire. Sixteenth century.

61 Pipkin in a cream-coloured hard fabric, trailed. Glazed of lead-yellow and copper-green round the rim. Sixteenth century.

62 Pipkin in a coarse brick-red fabric glazed inside and out to a light brown colour. Early seventeenth century.

63 Cup in a hard, red fabric, dark brown glaze inside and out. Seventeenth century.

64 Cup in a hard, red fabric with a black glaze to which had been added small patches of quartz crystal. Mid seventeenth century.

65 Cup in a creamy white fabric with an internal copper green glaze. Mid seventeenth century.

66 Tyg. Two-handled vessel in a hard, red fabric with a brown glaze. Late seventeenth century.

67 Plate. Trailed white slip pattern on a red earthenware base under a clear lead glaze. Late seventeenth into the eighteenth century.

68 Chamber pot. Brick-red earthenware under a clear lead glaze. Early eighteenth century.

addition of flint. The ware, which was thrown very carefully to give a uniform profile, was always oxidised. Such quality wares are mainly posset pots, loving cups, tankards and similar fine wares.

About this time also, combed slipware came into prominence. This form of black and yellow decoration began in the middle of the seventeenth century on small cups and drug pots as simple black dots on a white slipped body under a lead glaze, which gives a yellow and black pattern. By the end of the century the black decoration had altered from dots to stripes; many examples have the stripes stroked across at right angles, alternating one way and the other, to give what is known as a 'feathering' or 'combed' pattern. Such a pattern was seen to best advantage on circular plates and rectangular bread dishes. So popular was this form of decoration that it continued to be made right up to the beginning of the twentieth century.

Slip-decorated and undecorated earthenwares continued to be made to meet the growing home demand, determined by the now established industrial centres. Road, river and canal traffic were improving, to the extent that even inland potting centres such as Burslem could export in quantity to America. The variety of the wares produced is very considerable and in the main reached a high degree of competence by the middle of the eighteenth century, after which a rapid decline set in so that within fifty years fine traditional earthenwares vanished from the domestic scene. Coarse earthenwares, some of them slip-decorated, continued to be produced in some quantity and are commonplace but did not change much in shape right up to World War I, after which they suffered a considerable decline and were finished by the 1950s.

However, during this phase several important developments took place in two forms, technical and fabric.

In the technical field the development of kilns continued, and it appears that by the eighteenth century the multi-flue 'bottle' kiln was becoming universally adopted. Such kilns were also adapted for other industrial purposes, such as glasshouses and distilleries, and the form of them once established became fossilised and remained virtually unaltered right up to the middle of the present century when they ceased to be economical in the face of rising coal prices, the cost of labour, the march of mechanised potting and the anti-smoke laws.

The bottle kiln did not see the utter demise of the single- or double-flue kilns, which were still used at various places in England up to the end of the nineteenth century, and at Verwood, Wilts, a single-flue updraught kiln, loaded through a vent-hole, was in use up to the middle of the present century.

Another technical development of importance was the introduction of slip-casting, using a piece mould of 'biscuit', an unglazed fired body, or of plaster of paris. These methods, widely developed in the eighteenth century and still commonly used today, enable innumerable copies to be produced, and so a vessel and its component parts can be meticulously made. Throwing was not abandoned but greatly improved in quality during the second half of the eighteenth century. Leather-state 'engine turning' produced vessels of exquisite fineness and remarkable finish, and was highly prized in this first truly mechanical age.

From the end of the seventeenth century fabrics began to show a marked improvement at the hand of certain potters seeking the answer to the Chinese fine wares, which were offering so much competition. As the eighteenth century developed, not only Chinese tastes but the 'Grand Tour' began to show their influence. *Terra rubra* and *terra nigra* were in demand again after some 1,400 years.

The classical revival that spread through England from the mid to the late eighteenth century not only influenced architecture and furniture but also pottery; as a result, perhaps for the first time, ceramics acquired a 'snob' value. Not only were the wares of Rome and Egypt widely admired, but marbles, agates and coloured quartzes also became popular decorative media.

These foreign pottery forms and decorations were incorporated into the contemporary pottery designs and decoration in one form or another. Agate wares were produced by mixing multi-coloured clay bodies and turning the surface to show them to advantage when fired, or by applying a mixture of coloured slips to the surfaces. By the middle of the eighteenth century experiments to produce finer wares had become linked with the new ideas formulated by the stoneware potters and the ability to produce quality hard wares from high-temperature kilns. At this point the division between fine and coarse earthenwares divides sharply, for in the last twenty-five years of the eighteenth century we see rapid improvements. The search for finer and finer wares, although instigated by the desire to produce porcelain, eventually became a challenge to improve the results of the initial experiments. At this time there began a period of serious scientific research into the properties of pottery, the way was open for the genius of Wedgwood and his contemporaries, and it is from these researches plus the growing technical improvements of the factory system that the present ceramic industry has grown.

In the seventeenth and eighteenth centuries, the ceramic industry had facets other than pottery production. The introduction of tobacco at the end of the sixteenth century soon led to the production of clay tobacco pipes, and pipemakers are recorded as early as 1590. The manufacture of pipes using only a white ball clay required special techniques for piercing the stem and moulding the bowl. The pipes were fired in special clay trays. The kilns themselves—what is known of them—appear to have been small, rectangular structures, similar in form to parallel-flue kilns. The makers frequently marked their products with initials, or in some instances elaborate decorative motifs. Pipemaking continued in full flood up to the early part of this century, since when it has declined; in 1968 the Glasgow works closed down, leaving the ancient centre of production at Broseley making copies of eighteenth-century forms.

Pottery building materials continued in production from the time of their reintroduction in the Middle Ages, but by the seventeenth century this aspect of the ceramic industry had reached massive proportions. Bricks were fired in clamps, parallel-flue kilns and down-draught kilns. The material produced, although similar to that of the Middle Ages, was no longer decorated; it became dull and commonplace. There was a great surge in the use of such materials in the late eighteenth century, with the commencement of speculative building in the major towns, which carried right through to the dreadful red-brick period at the beginning of this century, since when, fortunately, there has been a reduction in the use of bricks, and new thought on their fabric and finish.

Building materials and heavy ceramics in general are the last preserve of earthenware, and the only remaining part of the trade where clay is still taken straight from the earth and worked to a product by methods whose traditions go back to the earliest times.

TIN-GLAZED EARTHENWARE

Known as maiolica or delft today, or as 'Gallypots' or 'painted earthenware' in the early phases of its introduction here, this ware is basically an earthenware with a refined fabric on which is a glaze made from lead, glass and tin which forms an enamel, so that it is also sometimes known as tin-enamel ware. Whatever the name, the object of the potter in making this ware was to provide a vessel with an all-over opaque glaze, which could be in a variety of colours, but which was predominantly white, and on this white surface to paint various decorations. As decoration was the main reason for the use of this form of earthenware, a good and where possible expansive surface was desired, so it could be said that tin-glazed earthenwares were 'plate-orientated', although a considerable number of other forms persisted; the greater part at least in the early phases were either just ornaments or 'best wares'.

This ware had a long history before it reached England. Its origins were probably in Syria, where it is known as early as the ninth century AD, and even there it is thought to have arisen as a direct result of the importation of Chinese porcelains. By the Middle Ages it was well established in Spain, Italy and southern France, and strangely enough did not spread inland at that time. The products of those countries were carried to England in small amounts, insufficient to have any profound effect on the local potters. By the late fifteenth century, however, it was coming in from Holland in increasing amounts, and by 1550 it was being produced here firstly by Flemish potters in Norwich, who then moved to London where the potteries of the south bank were founded. (The last kiln of ware fired at the south bank was of stoneware at Doultons, Lambeth, in August 1955.) From there during the succeeding century the manufacture of delft spread to Wincanton and to Bristol, and then to Liverpool, and finally in the eighteenth century to Glasgow, Belfast and Dublin.

The techniques required to fire the wares were more advanced than those of the incumbent pottery techniques. The preparation of the fabric required special care as it was required to become porous to take and seat the heavy layer of enamel that was to be fired on to it. The vessels were thrown or moulded, and then fired to a 'biscuit'. That is, they were fired without a glaze, and emerge from the kiln a dull uniform and predominantly buff colour. The biscuit was then dipped into the glaze and allowed to dry. When dry the opaque and very porous surface was decorated with a variety of patterns, using metal ores for colouring purposes, green from copper, purple and black from manganese and haematite, reds and browns from other iron ores, yellow from antimony, and sometimes a very rich red from gold, but the commonest colour was blue, made from cobalt. This use of a blue colour was the first time it had been seen on English pottery. Blue was made more popular as the period progressed, as it was also the commonest colour of the much-desired Chinese wares, which were also becoming more common during the late sixteenth century.

The wares, fired to biscuit, glazed and dried, decorated and dried again, were then 'glost' fired, and in this the use of the sagger came into prominence. Although we know of saggers being used in the late fifteenth century in the Yorkshire kilns, they were far from common before the inception of delft potting, after which they increased in use. These saggers, plain cylindrical vessels, had pegs fitted in the sides so that the dishes could be held on three points, and the traces of these supports can be seen on the bottom of most examples of this ware. The saggers when packed would be stacked in the kilns and fired. The control of both temperature and flame was important in the making of these wares because of the variety of metals used in decorations, and a muffle was introduced to prevent undue damage from the flames. The introduction of these wares thus brought added refinements to the technique of the industry, by the common use of saggers, a refined fabric, biscuit firing and muffle control.

The wares themselves began as straight copies of the types being made on the Continent, a variety of highly decorated maiolicas, in forms copying the continental vessels then being imported, although within fifty years anglicised decorations and shapes were already appearing. Early in the seventeenth century the art of copying Chinese patterns started on white vessels and the great 'blue and white delft' era had begun, an era that was to continue until the late eighteenth century. The subject of chinoiserie on delft is highly specialised and not one to be described in detail here, although it was common for some 130 years, there were a wide variety of forms and decorative motifs which developed in different ways. The English styles show themselves at intervals, and the most striking examples are the fine 'chargers', large dishes which bear representations of the monarch, or his consort, or of Adam and Eve, similar to those seen on the slipware dishes of the same period, which occur between 1660 and 1680. The pressure of porcelain manufacture in Europe, plus a torrent of imports of porcelain from China, seem to have driven the delftware potter into a frenzy of improvement and variation by the 1740s, and wide varieties of decorative forms are met with. The quality of some is extremely high. Also, from the turn of the eighteenth century, plain delft appears for ordinary domestic use, plates, bowls and chamber-pots being the commonest examples.

Despite the late establishment of the Scottish and Irish factories, the death-knell of the wares was sounded with the development of 'creamwares', and the introduction of home-produced porcelains in the 1760s, and delft manufacture declined very rapidly in the British Isles, to have passed away completely before 1800.

SALT-GLAZED STONEWARES

In 1671 a patent was granted for the manufacture of salt-glazed stonewares in England, yet such wares had been commonly imported to most parts of England since 1450.

Stoneware is pottery made from clay that can be fired to a high temperature until the body vitrifies. The method of making such wares had been developing throughout the Middle Ages in the Rhineland, where clay suitable for this purpose is abundant. Greater and greater temperatures were achieved and so the clay was gradually converted to what can be described as a vitrified rock-like structure which is impervious to water, as earthenware never was. From the fourteenth century it was found that the addition of salt to the fire at the highest point of the temperature caused the salt to volatilise, and the resultant sodium chloride vapour fluxed with the silicas in the body to form a soda-glass glaze. This radical change in providing a fine shiny cover was further embellished by providing a fine iron wash to the body before firing. Thus brown-glazed stoneware came into existence, and it was exported from Germany to the whole of Western Europe and beyond, through the ensuing centuries, in fantastic quantities. It is the commonest form of imported ware on archaeological sites occupied after 1450, and prominent amongst these wares are the famous Bellarmine jugs which proliferated during the last fifty years of the seventeenth century and into the eighteenth. This massive importation was met by some attempts to copy it in earthenware or imitate it in speckled delfts, but there is no evidence whatever of its being made here before the granting of the licence to manufacture in 1671.

The manufacturing techniques posed no specially new problems to those native potters who took up its manufacture.

The essential ingredients were a high-temperature body, and the means to produce a high temperature to fire it. Material for the former was readily available in this country, and the bottle kilns which could provide the temperature required were already established. Although it is known that some early salt-glazing was done in bottle kilns it is perhaps worth noting that by the late eighteenth century, and continuing to this day, down-draught kilns have been favoured for this work, not simply because the temperature was easily controlled, but because the act of salting the fire produces clouds of chlorine gas which is fatal if inhaled. By the down-draught method the gas was dispersed at some height from the work area.

The ware was not fired in biscuit, but when dried it was placed in a sagger, specially made with round or triangular holes to allow free passage of gas. The vessel was stood inside on a spread of sand. The process, then, is relatively simple and remains unchanged, as can be seen at potteries where land drains, Post Office telephone cable pipes, drains for carrying strong chemicals to waste, and similar materials are still produced at various places throughout England.

Why stoneware was not made here before the end of the seventeenth century will probably always remain a mystery, when so much else was being copied by one means or another. Whatever the reason, when salt-glazed stonewares were eventually made here, they were immediately revolutionised. Although in the very early stages we see the usual copies of imports by the home products, there occurred almost immediately an upsurge of new thought and the production of fine-quality white wares and sculpture of considerable artistic ability which matches well with any of the other figurative sculpture of that period. By the early eighteenth century, fine-quality table wares and ornaments were common products, and by this period the fine white wares were being embellished with sprigged decoration in either grey or green slips, or in high enamels, many of which accurately copied the Chinese enamelling. The cups and teapots imitated the Chinese wares. The tankards, which soon developed a character of their own, were to be a firmly established common drinking vessel up to the early nineteenth century. It is the plate, however, which epitomises the unique qualities of English salt-glaze. Many plates have the surface heavily moulded in the lace pattern of the period, and some are pierced elaborately. The use of blue, by this time common on porcelain and delft, was also applied to salt-glazed wares, some being straight copies of the now more elaborate German salt-glazed wares which continued to flood into the country. The quality of manufacture and decoration were of the highest order and frequently equalled, if they did not excel, that of the Chinese imports. Another factor in this aspect of the development was the production of fine, red-bodied stonewares imitating the Chinese wares of similar form, and, although relatively short-lived, this is important, as it led the way to the production of fine earthenwares. Salt-glazed stonewares of the finer variety then went into decline. It is certain that the way salt-glazed wares developed in this country between 1680 and 1720 gave potters an insight into the control of greater temperatures and led to the production of wares superior to those ever before made in Europe.

So by the 1750s we see the beginning of a completely new era in the history of English ceramics. The manufacture of porcelain has just begun, earthenwares are being refined away from their long-established patterns, lead-glazed earthenware is on the brink of decline, delft is battling gamely against the current, salt-glazed stonewares have pointed the way, and a whole new and wealthy period is just over the horizon. The next fifty years are to see changes never before experienced in such a short space of time in the whole history of English ceramics. Delft declines and vanishes from the scene, salt-glazed wares likewise; good-quality lead-glazed earthenwares fade slowly away, leaving only the coarsewares still in full flood. Fine earthenwares, stonewares and near-stonewares flourish and end up as common 'china'. Porcelain seems to have had its best days by 1800, but is with us still. Strange, isn't it, that the goal so many potters sought, and some fought and died for, and were litigated against and ruined because of, the elusive porcelain, never became as popular as the wares ultimately derived from humble earthenware beginnings?

Bibliography

PREHISTORIC

The Journals of the county archaeological societies, principally those of: Dorset, Norfolk, Wiltshire and Yorkshire. For Neolithic and early Bronze Age parallels: *Journal of The Royal Society of Ireland*

Annable, K. and Simpson, D. D. A. *Guide Catalogue of the Neolithic and Bronze Age Collections in Devizes Museum*, Wiltshire Archaeological and Natural History Society (1964)

Calkin, J. Bernard. 'The Bournemouth Area in the Middle and Late Bronze Age with the Deveral Rimbury Problem Reconsidered', *The Archaeological Journal*, cxix (1964)

English Prehistoric Pottery, Victoria & Albert Museum (HMSO, 1952)

Fox, Sir Cyril. *Life and Death in the Bronze Age* (1959)

Guide to Early Iron Age Antiquities, British Museum (1925)

Hawkes, C. and Hull, M. 'Camulodunum', *Society of Antiquaries Research Report* (1947)

Hodson, F. R. 'Some Pottery from Eastbourne: The "Marnians" and the pre-Roman Iron Age in Southern England', *Proceedings of the Prehistoric Society*, xxviii (1962)

—— 'Cultural Grouping within the British pre-Roman Iron Age', *Proceedings of the Prehistoric Society* (1964)

Kenyon, Kathleen M. 'A Survey of the Evidence Concerning the Chronology and Origins of the Iron Age "A" in Southern and Midland Britain', *Institute of Archaeology Eighth Annual Report* (1952)

Piggott, Stuart. 'The Early Bronze Age in Wessex', *Proceedings of the Prehistoric Society* (1938)

The Proceedings of the Prehistoric Society

Smith, I. F. 'Windmill Hill and Its Implications', *Palaeohistoria*, 12 (1966)

Wheeler, E. M. 'Maiden Castle, Dorset', *Society of Antiquaries Research Report* (1943)

Bibliography

ROMAN

Journals: *Britannia!*, Journal of Romano-British Archaeology; *The Journal of Roman Studies*; and all county archaeological journals

Annable, F. K. *The Romano-British Pottery at Cantley Housing Estate, Doncaster*, Museum and Art Gallery, Doncaster (1960)

Collingwood, R. G., and Richmond, Ian *The Archaeology of Roman Britain* (1969)

Corder, Philip. 'A Romano-British Pottery Kiln on the Lincoln Racecourse', *Department of Adult Education, University of Nottingham* (1950)

—— 'The Roman Town and Villa at Great Casterton, Rutland, *University of Nottingham* (1951)

Detsicas, A. 'Current Research in Romano-British Coarse Pottery', *Council for British Archaeology Research Report No 10* (1973)

Frere, Shepard. *Britannia* (1967)

Gillam, J. P. 'Types of Roman Coarse Pottery Vessels in Northern Britain', *Archaeologia Aeliana*, xxxv (1957)

Hull, M. R. 'The Roman Potters Kilns of Colchester', *Society of Antiquaries Research Report* (1963)

Hume, I. Noël. 'Romano-British Potteries on the Upchurch Marshes', *Archaeologica Cantiana*, lxviii (1954)

Kenyon, Kathleen. 'The Jewry Wall Site, Leicester', *Society of Antiquaries Research Report* (1948)

Oswald, F. and Pryce, T. D. *Terra Sigillata* (1920)

Passmore, Anthony. *New Forest Pottery Kilns and Earthworks* (1968)

Rogers, G. and Laing, L. R. 'Gallo-Roman Pottery from Southampton and the Distribution of Terra Nigra in Britain', *Southampton City Museums Publication No 6* (1966)

Webster, Graham. 'A Note on Romano-British Pottery with Painted Figures', *The Antiquaries Journal*, xxxix (1959)

Webster, Graham (ed). 'Romano-British Coarse Pottery—A Students Guide', *Council for British Archaeology Research Report No 6* (undated)

ROMANO-SAXON, DARK AGES AND PAGAN SAXONS

County archaeological journals (Dark Ages): Cornwall, Devon, Somerset, Wales. County archaeological journals (Pagan Saxons): Essex, Hampshire, Kent, Lincoln, Norfolk, Suffolk, Sussex. Periodicals as for the Romano-British period; and *Medieval Archaeology*

'Anglo-Saxon Symposium', *Medieval Archaeology*, iii (1959)

Arthur, B. V. and Jope, E. M. 'Early Saxon Pottery Kilns at Purwell Farm, Cassington, Oxfordshire', *Medieval Archaeology*, vi-vii (1962-3)

Bibliography

Barton, K. J. 'Settlements of the Iron Age and Pagan Saxon Periods at Linford, Essex', *Essex Archaeological Society* (1956)

Cunliffe, Barry. 'The Saxon Culture Sequence at Porchester', *The Antiquaries Journal*, l (1970)

Fox, Aileen. 'Some Evidence for a Dark Age Trading Site at Bantham, Near Thurlestone, South Devon', *The Antiquaries Journal*, xxxv (1955)

Guide to Anglo-Saxon Antiquities, British Museum (1923)

Harden, D. B. (ed). *Dark Age Britain* (1955)

Hayes, J. W. 'Late Roman Pottery', *The British School at Rome* (1972)

Myres, J. N. L. 'The Anglo-Saxon Pottery of Lincolnshire' (both), *The Archaeological Journal*, cviii (1952)

—— *Anglo-Saxon Pottery and The Settlement of England* (1969)

Webster, Graham. 'An Anglo-Saxon Urnfield at South Elkington, South Lincolnshire'. *The Archaeological Journal*, cviii (1952)

MIDDLE SAXON, LATE SAXON AND SAXO-NORMAN WARES

Principal county journals: Cheshire, Essex, Gloucester, Hampshire, Herefordshire, Lincoln, Norfolk, Suffolk, Yorkshire. *Medieval Archaeology* and *The Antiquaries Journal* since 1964 for interim reports on excavations by M. Biddle of Winchester and B. Cunliffe at Porchester

Addyman, P. 'A Saxo-Norman Kiln Producing Stamped Wares at Michelmersh, Hants'. *Medieval Archaeology*, xvi (1972)

Cramp, Rosemary. 'Excavations at the Saxon Monastic Sites of Wearmouth and Jarrow', The Pottery, by J. G. Hurst, *Medieval Archaeology*, xiii (1969)

Hebditch, M. G. 'A Saxo-Norman Kiln Discovered in Southgate Street, Leicester, 1964', *Leicester Archaeological Society*, xliii (1967-8)

Hurst, J. G. 'Saxo-Norman Pottery in East Anglia'. Part one: St Neots ware: part two: Thetford Ware and Middle Saxon Ipswich Ware; part three: Stamford Ware. *Proceedings of the Cambridge Archaeological Society*, xlix (1956), l (1957), li (1958)

Jope, E. M. 'Late Saxon Pits Under Oxford Castle Mound: Excavations 1952', *Oxoniensia*, xvii/xviii (1952-3)

Kennett, D. H. 'St Neots Ware from Bedford: Jugs and Bowls', *Bedfordshire Archaeological Journal*, iv (1969)

MEDIEVAL

Journals: All county journals; and *Medieval Archaeology*

Barton, K. J. 'The Medieval Pottery of Worcester', *Transactions of the Worcestershire Archaeological Society*, 1 (1965-7)

—— 'The Medieval Pottery of Sussex'. A thesis deposited at Southampton University, publication forthcoming

Bibliography

Cunliffe, Barry. *Winchester Excavations*, vol 1. City of Winchester (1964)

Davidson, Brian K. 'Castle Neroche an Abandoned Norman Fortress in South Somerset', *Somerset Archaeological and Natural History Society*, 116 (1972)

Dunning, G. C. and Wilson, A. E. 'Late Saxon and Early Medieval Pottery from Selected Sites in Chichester', *Sussex Archaeological Collections*, xci (1953)

Dunning, G. C. 'Medieval Chimney Pots', *Studies in Building History* (1961)

—— 'The Pottery Louvre from Goosegate, Nottingham', *Transactions of the Thoroton Society of Nottingham* (1962)

—— 'A Medieval Pottery Roof Ventilator from Weybread', *Proceedings of the Suffolk Institute of Archaeology*, xxx (1966)

Eames, Elizabeth S. *Medieval Tiles*, British Museum (1968)

Fox, Aileen and Dunning, G. C. 'A Medieval Pottery Kiln in Exeter', *The Antiquaries Journal*, xxxvii (1957)

Gardner, J. S. and Eames, Elizabeth. 'A Tile Kiln at Chertsey, Surrey', *Journal of the British Archaeological Association*, xvii (1954)

Jope, E. M. 'Medieval Pottery in Berkshire', *Berkshire Archaeological Journal*, 50 (1947)

—— 'Regional Character in West Country Pottery', *Bristol and Gloucester Archaeological Society*, 71 (1952)

—— 'The Clarendon Hotel, Oxford, Part 1', *Oxoniensia*, xxiii (1958)

Jope, E. M. and Threlfall, R. I. 'The Twelfth-century Castle at Ascot Doilly, Oxfordshire', *The Antiquaries Journal*, xxxix (1959)

Kennet, David. *Early Medieval Pottery in the Nene Valley*, Northampton Museums (1968)

Marshall, C. 'A Medieval Kiln Discovered at Cheam', *Surrey Archaeological Collections*, xxxv (1924)

Millard, Louise. 'Some Medieval Pottery from North Bucks', *Record of Bucks*, xviii (1967)

Musty, John (*et al*). 'The Medieval Pottery Kilns at Laverstock, Wiltshire', *Archaeologia*, cii (1969)

Rackham, B. '*Medieval English Pottery* (1972)

Rutter, J. G. 'Medieval Pottery in the Scarborough Museum', *Scarborough and District Archaeological Society* (1961)

Stebbing, P. J., Spillett, W. P. D. and Dunning, G. C. 'A Pottery Kiln Site at Tyler Hill Near Canterbury', *Archaeologia Cantiana*, lv (1947)

Truckell, A. E. and Williams, J. 'Medieval Pottery in Dumfriesshire and Galloway', *The Transactions of the Dumfriesshire and Galloway Natural History Society*, xlvi (1967)

139

Bibliography

Webster, Graham and Dunning, Gerald. 'A Medieval Pottery Kiln at Audlem, Cheshire', *Medieval Archaeology*, iv (1960)

POST-MEDIEVAL UP TO THE EIGHTEENTH CENTURY

Journals: Some county journals; *Post-Medieval Archaeology;* and *Medieval Catalogue*, London Museums (1972 2nd ed)

Archer, M. *English Delftware in the Robert Hall Warren Collection* (1968)

Barton, K. J. 'Buckley Potteries, Excavations at Prescotts Pottery', *Flintshire Historical Society Publications*, 16 (1956)

—— 'Some Evidence for Two Types of Pottery Manufactured in Bristol in the Early Eighteenth Century', *Bristol and Gloucester Archaeological Society*, 80 (1961)

—— 'The Excavations of a Medieval Bastion at St Nicholas' Alms Houses, King Street, Bristol', *Medieval Archaeology*, viii (1964)

Bemrose, G. *Nineteenth Century English Pottery and Porcelain* (1952)

Brears, P. J. 'A Catalogue of English Country Pottery', *Yorkshire Philosophical Society* (1968)

—— *The English Country Pottery* (1971)

—— *The Farnham Potteries*, Farnham Museum (1972)

Celoria, Francis. *Dated Post-Medieval Pottery*, London Museum (1966)

Cooper, R. G. *English Slipware Dishes* 1650-1850 (1968)

Fennelly, L. R. (*et al*). 'A Late Medieval Kiln at Knighton', *Hampshire Field Club and Archaeological Society*, xxvi (1969)

Garner, F. H. and Archer, M. *English Delftware* (1972 2nd ed)

Holling, F. W. 'Seventeenth Century Pottery from Ash, Surrey', *Post-Medieval Archaeology*, 3 (1969)

—— 'A Preliminary Note on the Pottery Industry of the Hampshire —Surrey Border', *The Surrey Archaeological Collections*, lxvii (1971)

The Journals of Ceramic History (from 1968)

Kelly, D. B. 'An Early Tudor Kiln at Hareplain, Biddenden, Kent', *Archaeologica Cantiana*, lxxxviii (1972)

Lloyd, Nathaniel. *A History of English Brickwork*, H. Greville Montgomery (1925)

Mayes, P. and Pirie, Elizabeth. 'A Cistercian Ware Kiln of the Early Sixteenth Century at Potterton Yorkshire', *The Antiquaries Journal*, xlvi (1966)

Moorehouse, Stephen. 'Some Finds From Basing House Hampshire, 1540-1645, part one', *Post-Medieval Archaeology*, 4 (1970)

Morgan, F. C. 'Herefordshire Potteries', *Woolhope Naturalists Field Club*, xxxv (1956)

Mynard, D. C. 'A Group of Post-Medieval Pottery from Dover Castle', *Post-Medieval Archaeology*, 3 (1969)

Newton, E. F. and Bibbings, E. 'Seventeenth Century Pottery Sites at Harlow, Essex', *Essex Archaeological Society*, xxv (1960)

Bibliography

Oswald, Adrian. 'The Archaeology and History of English Clay Tobacco Pipes', *Journal of the Archaeological Association*, xxiii (1960)
The Proceedings of the English Ceramic Circle
Rackham, B. *Catalogue of the Glaisher Collection in the Fitzwilliam Museum* (1935)
—— 'Farnham Pottery of the Sixteenth Century', *Surrey Archaeological Collections*, lii (1952)
The Reports of the City of Stoke-on-Trent Archaeological Society (from 1964)
Solon, M. L. *The Art of the Old English Potter* (1885)
Talbot, Eric J. 'Welsh Ceramics: a Documentary and Archaeological Survey', *Post-Medieval Archaeology*, 2 (1968)
Watkins, C. Malcolm. 'North Devon Pottery and Its Export to America in the Seventeenth Century', *US National Museum Bulletin*, 225 (1960)
Webster, Graham and Barton, K. J. 'An Eighteenth-century Rubbish Pit from Trinity Street, Chester', *Chester and District Archaeological Society*, 44 (1957).
Wells, P. K. 'The Excavation of a Nineteenth-century Clay Tobacco Pipe Kiln at Boston, Lincolnshire', *Lincolnshire History and Archaeology*, 1 (1970)

Glossary

ACERAMIC   A culture not using pottery.

ANGLO-NIPPONESE   Pottery made by Bernard Leach and his school which is a mélange of English traditions in stoneware fabrics with oriental glazes. A twentieth-century phenomenon.

ARCHAEOLOGICAL TIME SCALE

Neolithic (New Stone Age), 2500–2000 BC
Bronze Age, 2000–600 BC
Iron Age, 600 BC to AD 43
Romano-British period, AD 43–450
Saxon, AD 450–1000
Medieval, AD 1000–1450
Post-medieval, AD 1450–1750
Recent 1750 +

Sub-periods
Beaker period   =   early Bronze Age
Hallstatt   =   early Iron Age
La Tène   =   middle Iron Age
Belgic   =   late Iron Age
Romano-Saxon =   fourth and fifth centuries AD
Pagan-Saxon   =   fifth to seventh centuries AD
Late Saxon   =   seventh to ninth centuries AD
Saxo-Norman   =   tenth to twelfth centuries AD
Late medieval or early post-medieval   =   late fifteenth to sixteenth centuries AD

BARREL VAULT   Semicircular sectioned roof built of Voussoir bricks.

BEAD RIM   A rounded rim section.

BEAKER   A drinking cup of special cultural significance in the early Bronze Age.

Glossary

BISCUIT Unglazed ware, or ware fired unglazed preparatory to glazing. Different temperatures are needed for glaze than for biscuit firing, so for decorated pieces this is the most economical process.

BLUNGING Reducing clay to a workable consistency by working with feet or hands or by slicing with a wire and casting the cut pieces at each other, which is known as wedging.

BURNISHING Polishing the vessel while it is in a leather state.

CASTING Slip poured into a two-part mould to form a vessel.

CERAMIC A piece of clay converted to pottery by firing to a temperature of not less than 500°C.

CISTERCIAN WARES Late fifteenth-century brownwares of North Midland/South Yorkshire origin.

COLOUR-COATED The use of slips with a high metal content to give a colour to the vessel's surface.

CREAMWARE A refined earthenware, produced in quantity in the middle to late eighteenth century, originally by Wedgwood, subsequently and in quantity at the South Yorkshire potteries.

DELFT Earthenware with a glaze of lead heavily filled with tin to create a white ground suited to decoration. Also known as tin-glazed earthenware.

FINIAL A ceramic ornament of very individualistic design set on top of the gable in the medieval and post-medieval periods.

FOOD VESSELS A type of small vessel which copies larger types of the same period found in graves in the early Bronze Age.

FRISIAN Pertaining to Frisia, a country now in the north of the Netherlands.

GALENA An ore of lead.

GLAZING The act of putting glass on the outside of a pottery vessel for decoration or to attempt to make the vessel impervious to water. This can be achieved by lead or a lead/tin/zinc combination or at low temperatures or by wood ash or other soda ashes or by salt at high temperatures.

GLOST FIRING A potter's term for firing glazed wares or for the kiln in which they are fired.

GREEN A formed and partially dried pot ready for decoration or burnishing, also known as 'in leather state'.

GROG A tempering agent made from a crushed ceramic product.

HAEMATITE A red or brown ore of iron.

HEARTH FURNITURE Oven tiles, oven bricks, ovens.

HOVEL The workshop built round a kiln where pottery is dried prior to firing.

INCENSE CUPS Small funerary cup-like vessels the true purpose of which is unknown.

KILN TYPES
> *Clamp kiln*
> An archaeological term for a suggested method of firing pottery without a structure in an open fire.
>
> *Single-flue updraught*
> One stoke-hole into the firing chamber; the gas expelled upwards.
>
> *Double-flue updraught*
> Two stoke-holes into the firing chamber; the gas expelled upwards.
>
> *Multi-flue updraught*
> More than two stoke-holes into the firing chamber; the gas expelled upwards.
>
> *Bottle kiln*
> A refined version of the mult-flue kiln but a permanent structure built of bricks; these can go up to 100ft in height. The gas expelled upwards.
>
> *Down-draught kiln*
> A version of the multi-flue kiln in which the draught is drawn downwards through the kiln by virtue of a tall chimney to which it is connected by a tunnel.
>
> *Parallel-flue kiln*
> A rectangular structure with a slatted floor under which are two or more parallel tunnels, the heat being drawn through these tunnels and the gas expelled upwards. A permanent or semi-permanent structure.

LEATHER STATE *See* GREEN

LOUVERS A ceramic vent fitting on the roof tree heavily decorated with zoomorphic designs, occurring in the medieval and post-medieval periods.

LUTING Joining two pieces of unfired clay with slip as the adhesive.

MORTAR A heavy dish with gravel set on the insides used for grinding food.

PETERBOROUGH WARE A late Neolithic pottery style named after the type site.

PORCELAIN Highly developed translucent stoneware made of a mixture of kaolin and other siliceous material.

PRESS MOULDING Clay pressed into a mould and allowed to dry, the segments joined together by luting.

ROMANO-BRITISH Artifacts or structures made or used between AD 43–450.

ROOF FURNITURE Flat tiles, ridge tiles, valley tiles, hip tiles, chimney pots, ventilators, louvers and finials.

SAGGER A pottery container in which glazed vessels are placed to separate them from others.

SAMIAN (*terra sigilata*) A red, colour-coated, spin-moulded ware made usually in northern Italy and France during the Roman period.

SILICATE A compound of silica, in this case with an alumina base.

SITULAE A name given to bucket-shaped pots of late Bronze Age and Iron Age date.

SLIP Clay mixed with water until it is thin and creamy.

SPIN MOULDING Throwing clay into a mould and spinning it into shape.

SPRIGGING Moulding small decorations which are then luted on to the vessel.

STONEWARE A ware fired to a high temperature causing the body to become vitrified and therefore impervious to liquid penetration. This ware is frequently covered with an iron wash, then glazed by adding salt at the maximum temperature to provide a hard and shiny glaze.

TEMPERING The addition of material to leaven the clay and thereby make it easier to fire at a lower temperature.

TERRA NIGRA A black, reduced, sometimes colour-coated ware.

TERRA RUBRA An oxidised and therefore red ware, sometimes achieved by colour-coating.

TURNTABLE A non-mechanical revolving surface.

VOUSSOIR BRICK A brick shaped with a tapering end, designed to make an arch.

WALK-IN The door to a multi-flue kiln.

WASTER HEAP A by-product of any pottery industry.

WASTERS A potter's term for all material that was not saleable.

WEDGWOOD Pottery made by the firm founded by Josiah Wedgwood (1730–95).

WHIPPED CORD A term used to describe the decoration found on vessels from the late Neolithic period to the late Bronze Age made by impressing cord or string on the side of the vessel.

ZOOMORPHIC In the form of animals.

Index

Page references in italic refer to illustrations

Index